Also Published by Ballantine Books:

BARRY MANILOW
BILLY IDOL
BILLY JOEL
BRUCE SPRINSTEEN
CULTURE CLUB
CYNDI LAUPER
DURAN DURAN
EURYTHMICS
HALL AND OATES
HUEY LEWIS AND THE NEWS
JOHN COUGAR MELLENCAMP
JULIAN LENNON
THE PRETENDERS
PRINCE
STEVIE NICKS
STEVIE WONDER
STING AND THE POLICE
TINA TURNER
VAN HALEN
WHAM!
ZZ TOP

U2

Winston Brandt

All rights reserved under International and Pan-American Copyright Conventions. Published in the United States of America by Ballantine Books, a division of Random House, Inc., New York, and simultaneously in Canada by Random House of Canada Limited, Toronto.

Library of Congress Catalog Card Number: 86-90836

ISBN 0-345-32892-1

First Edition: January 1986

Cover photographs by David Michael Kennedy

A 2M Communications Production

BALLANTINE BOOKS • NEW YORK

Library of Congress Catalog Card Number: 85-90856

ISBN 0-345-32892-2

Manufactured in the United States of America

First Edition. January 1986

Front Cover photo: David Montgomery, Robert Montgomery
& Partners
Back Cover photo: Gene Kirkland/Thunder Thumbs
Photo Research: Amanda Rubin
Interior Design: Michaelis/Carpelis Design Associates, Inc.

CONTENTS

ACKNOWLEDGMENTS

Many people and organizations helped me with this book. I'd like to give special thanks to the following ones:

The staff of the Progressive Radio Network, Ed Steinberg and the staff of Rockamerica, Mark Josephson and the staff of Rockpool, Virginia Lohle of Star File, Bob Haber and the staff of the *College Media Journal*, David Keeps and the staff of *Star Hits* magazine, Ted Oljewoski, the staff of ProMedia, Binky Phillips, Chuck Pulin, Eric Levin, Chris Willman, John Neilson, John Gibson of the *Irish Times*, Kevin Knapp, Michael Duff, Richard Sweret, the people at It's Only Rock 'n' Roll, Jim Green, Tim Summer, Madeleine Morel, Karen Moline, and the many other people who freely shared their time, knowledge, and memories with me.

INTRODUCTION

*T*wenty thousand people pack the auditorium. Onstage a solitary musician clumsily strums a chord, and the crowd erupts. As the backup band joins in, the cheers grow louder, the music swells, and the mammoth hall becomes an intimate room filled with joyous loving friends.

Why is the crowd going wild? There's nothing special about the man in the spotlight. Anybody could be up there playing the guitar like that—even you.

That's the point U2 wants to make. That's why they've brought one of their fans onstage. Why, at the pinnacle of rock stardom, they invite the audience to share their glory. It's a simple demonstration of everything U2 believes in: that music should unite people, not separate them; that anything you set your mind to, you can do.

And all across the world, people take the message to heart. From Sydney to Stockholm, from Texas to Tokyo, people respond to U2 with a feeling of love no other group in the world can evoke. It's a love and a passion that U2's platinum-selling albums and sold-out stadiums can only begin to measure, that their tremendous musical talent only partly explains.

This is the story of four friends possessed with a belief in themselves, their destiny, and the power of music.

It's the story of four schoolboys who couldn't even play instruments and went on to become perhaps the most important band in the world. Four youngsters who should have known better, who wouldn't listen when people said their dreams were impossible, who refused to let adversity stand in their way. Four people who grew up surrounded by hatred and responded with love. Four individuals who feel their success belongs to everyone, that their triumph is the triumph of the human spirit.

It's not the story of rock 'n' roll revelry, egos, and excess. It's no more or less than the story of the four people, the four friends now onstage who've temporarily given up the spotlight so that it may shine on everyone.

This is the story of U2.

STORIES FOR
BOYS

U_2 is an Irish band. That doesn't mean they grew up in the land of blarney and leprechauns; it means they grew up in the shadow of devastating religious and political strife, where, a few miles to the north of their Dublin roots, a youngster's more likely to be cut down by bullets or a bomb than form a rock 'n' roll band.

They call it the Troubles, the violence that splits Ireland in two as much the physical border divides it into north and south, the Republic of Ireland and Northern Ireland. Northern Ireland is controlled by England, and the British occupation is contested by its Catholic minority. The Protestants have religious and historical links to the English, and it's the struggle between these two groups that rips the country apart.

It's hard for anyone growing up surrounded by this hatred to escape the barriers separating Catholics and Protestants. The Hewsons managed to. He was a Catholic postal investigator and accomplished amateur artist. She was a Protestant.

On May 10, 1960, Paul, their second son, was born. He grew up in Ballymun, a solid, middle-class area in Dublin. It was a neighborhood where people grew up, got a job, got married, had children, and died. Most of the time in between was spent in pubs, as Paul observed later.

He and his mates, some of them the neighborhood toughs, vowed to avoid the kind of life they saw around them and spent most of their time playing elaborate but harmless pranks and creating group fantasies to get away from the depressing reality surrounding them.

Village People

Paul and his gang invented a make-believe kingdom called Lypton Village. It was a place where someone could be whatever he wanted, larger than life, where a boy's future was as wide open as his imagination. One of the rites of citizenship in Lypton Village was getting a nickname, a new identity as different from the dull life of Ballymun as possible. There was Clive Whistling Fellow, Guck Pants Delaney, Man-of-Strength Arran, and Little Biddy One-Way Street.

Paul was dubbed Bono Vox of O'Connell Street, compliments of a neighbor across the street whom Bono promptly named Guggi. Paul's nickname was later shortened to Bono Vox, but he still wasn't very pleased with it and even tried to get people to call him Paul Vox.

"We said, 'Don't be stupid, Bono's a really good name— Bono Vox.' And eventually, what's natural you just have to accept."

This memory is provided by a former Lyptonite who'd been dubbed Gavin Friday, a Dublin musician and friend of Bono's who still uses his Lypton Village name.

To this day, Bono's friends, even Guggi, claim they're not quite sure where the name Bono Vox came from, but there are a couple of intriguing suggestions. Here they are:

1. Bono's always been someone who loves to talk, mainly because he loves to communicate. To his friends, this meant he was a loudmouth. In Latin, Bono Vox means "good voice," and the name may

have been a left-handed compliment to Bono's vocal performances long before he began to sing.
2. Bono Vox is the brand name of an old English hearing aid—just the thing you wouldn't need as long as the person named Bono Vox was around. Unless, of course, he talked your ear off!

Wherever it came from, the name stuck, though years later he shortened it to just plain Bono. When pronounced properly, it rhymes with "mono," as in the opposite of stereo. (Don't confuse it with the last name of Cher's former husband.)

Not all the Lyptonites were from Ballymun, nor were they all loud and wisecracking. In fact, one of Bono's best friends was a rather quiet, reserved, even dignified youngster who lived in the more affluent Dublin neighborhood of Malahide Village, a bit to the north. His name was Dave Evans, and of course, Bono had to come up with a nickname: He was dubbed the Edge.

Ask Bono how he came up with the name, and he's apt to grab Edge by the chin, pointing to his angular profile, and simply proclaim, "The Edge!" He's also referred to his childhood friend as "a man of angles. He's got his chin, guitar, and elbows." Nowadays the names the Edge and just plain Edge are used interchangeably.

And then there was Adam Clayton. Not being a true local lad, he wasn't an official Lyptonite, but eventually he became a good friend of Bono's, the Edge, and the rest of the gang. Adam had been born in a village outside of Oxford, near London, but spent his early years in the colony of Tanganyika, in Africa (his father was an RAF pilot). In 1964 Adam turned four and Tanganyika became the independent nation of Tanzania. The Claytons moved to Dublin, and Adam's father got a job as a pilot for British Airways.

But Adam had trouble fitting in. A real nonconformist, he bounced from one school to the next. And, his parents noted with alarm, he was hanging around with the local toughs. If he kept up this way, what was to become of him?

Yet while adults saw nothing but trouble in this group, there was one aspect of Lypton Village that was remarkably positive: It was totally free of the religious strife permeating the Irish consciousness. The Lyptonites didn't pay much attention to organized religion at all. From what they could see, religion seemed to be a source of suffering, not salvation.

Soon Ballymun wasn't big enough. They branched out into downtown Dublin, where they staged what can only be described in retrospect as performance art. Using props they dragged from home—electric drills, saws, hoses, brooms—they created spontaneous theater pieces, making up dialogue and whatever passed for plot as they went along. They were, as Bono described it, "a gang of nut cases."

Growing Problems

What would happen to the kids from Ballymun as they reached their teens? How much longer could the pranks continue before getting them into real trouble?

These doubts followed Bono and Adam into the Mount Temple Comprehensive School. Edge, who also was sent to Mount Temple, wasn't much cause for worry. He was an academic whiz, following in the footsteps of his father, an engineer who worked out of the family garage, designing industrial heating and cooling systems.

Lying two miles to the north of the heart of Dublin, on Malahide Road, Mount Temple Comprehensive School is set on twenty-three acres. It's dominated by a large two-story nineteenth-century building formerly the center of the estate the school was carved from, and now surrounded by modern classroom additions.

A "comprehensive school" means high school. But Mount Temple isn't an ordinary high school by either Irish or American standards. In Ireland most high schools are private parochial schools, divided not just by religion but by gender as well. Mount Temple has 760 Protestant and Catholic students, boys and girls, rich and poor, all mixing together. What sets it apart from many American high schools is that educational activities outside the standard curriculum are stressed and encouraged.

When Bono started at Mount Temple, his extracurricular interests included little more than hanging around with his friends from Ballymun, thumbing his nose at the more conventional inhabitants of Dublin. He was an indifferent student yet exhibited a streak of stubborn intelligence accompanying his restlessness. While others studied the required Gaelic, the traditional Irish tongue, Bono refused. Instead, he read German books in class.

"I was pretty hard-headed and I thought, 'This language is dead. Why am I learning something that's dead?'"

Banding Together

At the age of fifteen, Bono was subjected to a traumatic experience that had a profound influence on his life. His mother died, and her sudden passing shattered not only Bono but his father and brother, too. Mr. Hewson packed up his canvases and pigments and never picked up a brush again. He tried keeping the household together for the sake of his sons, but Bono didn't make the job any easier. His mother's death filled him with rage, and it spilled over into his life at school and with his mates. Where he had been lackadaisical about studying, he now became disruptive. Where his escapades with the Lyptonites had always been essentially harmless, they now took on a more violent edge.

At home there were constant fights with his older brother. "I was such a bastard," Bono confessed, looking back on those dark days. Bono still thinks there may still be blood on the kitchen wall bearing testimony to their physical confrontations. The peak of his rage came when he hurled a knife at his brother.

Fortunately, it missed the mark and may have been responsible for forcing Bono to take a long look at himself and at life. He saw the tremendous fortitude his father showed in trying to keep the family together. And he took a harder look at his Ballymun mates. "I felt we were laughing at the same jokes as the years went by, and I backed off."

Despite the determination they'd all expressed to avoid becoming like everyone else, he saw a growing number of his mates falling into that very trap, wasting their talents and abilities, settling for the menial jobs they swore they'd never take. Some were getting into drugs and alcohol; others were dying. More than ever, he was determined not to let that happen to him.

"When you see somebody who has so much end up with so little, that can really upset you," he reflected.

Gradually his rage and confusion were replaced by a growing religious conviction. Not in the Irish sense of Catholic or Protestant but in the belief in a power supreme to all others, a power bigger than the demarcations of conventional religious denominations.

Yet he was still possessed by the tremendous energy and spirit that made him a natural leader among his friends. He just needed to find a positive outlet for it.

Bono may have pondered this situation as he walked to Larry Mullen's house late in 1976. Some days earlier, Larry had posted a notice on the bulletin board at Mount Temple, looking for people interested in starting a band. Normally Bono wouldn't have much to do with Mullen, being ahead of him in school. But Bono heard Edge and Adam Clayton had gotten together with Larry, and starting a band sounded like something interesting to do.

"I suppose the first link in the chain," as Edge remembered how he came to the band, "was a visit to the local jumble sale where I purchased a guitar for a pound. That was my first instrument. It was an acoustic guitar and me and my elder brother Dick both played it, plonking away, all very rudimentary stuff, open chords and all that.

"The next stage was a note on the school board to the effect that Larry had wasted a lot of money on drums and was interested in finding other people to waste money on guitars and stuff like that."

Larry Mullen was a quiet student at Mount Temple, but he stuck out anyway. Even at fourteen, with his smoky good looks and shy grace, he was an unreachable heart-throb to many of his female classmates. His fondness for leather jackets and long hair made him seem rebellious. In fact, his refusal to get a haircut got him bounced from the Artane Boys' Band, a school-affiliated marching band. The notice on the bulletin board was his answer.

Larry had taken up the drums because, as he said later, he realized he was "a very aggressive person, in a positive sense. I liked to hit things. Playing drums was the only thing I could do." He certainly wasn't going to let being canned from the marching band stop him from playing.

When Bono got to Larry's house that afternoon, Edge and Adam were already there. They made an interesting pair. As reserved and thoughtful as Edge was, Adam was impulsive and flashy. He had already acquired a reputation as Mount Temple's resident hell-raiser. He drank coffee in class and was likely to show up for school dressed in a kilt or a fur coat, or be seen running down the hallways wearing nothing at all.

One day the headmaster, Mr. Medlycott, who still runs the school, found himself in a discussion with a faculty member about Adam's future at Mount Temple—whether he could be rehabilitated or expelled. After finally reaching the conclusion that there was hope for him, they heard a branch snap and turned to see Adam fall from the tree outside the headmaster's window, where he'd secretly perched to overhear the discussion of his fate.

"I wasn't prepared for the establishment to write me off just because I didn't fit into their academic concept," he observed in hindsight.

At Larry's, everyone gathered in the kitchen, where Larry had his drum kit set up. Edge's older brother Dick was also there. Larry, being the one responsible for getting everyone together, was doing his best to provide leadership, even though he was the youngest. At the first couple of meetings, everyone deferred to him. It was his kitchen, and no one else had any real idea of what to do. Until the afternoon Bono showed up.

As Larry later reported, "I had two days of glory when I was tellin' people what to do. Then Bono came in and that was the end. He took it from there."

Yet Larry made a strong impression on Bono. He later remembered how during that first rehearsal several young girls were literally climbing the walls that surrounded Larry's house, trying to catch a glimpse of the cute young drummer. Larry would shout at them to go away, but they kept coming back and peeking in the window. Finally Larry went outside and turned the garden hose on them. The boys were left to discuss the band's future in peace.

There were a lot of decisions to be made. What kind of band would they be? What songs would they play? Where would they get equipment, and where would they play? And there was one other rather important matter to contend with—other than Larry, and the Edge's tinkering on guitar, none of them could play an instrument!

Not that they all let on. Adam's fleeting association with a rock band hadn't taught him how to play, but he had acquired an amplifier. He dropped all kinds of lingo like "gig," "fret," and "action" (the height of the strings above the neck of the guitar). Based on these buzz words, the others were convinced he was some kind of virtuoso.

Adam's reasons for joining the band were pretty simple. As he recalled, he spent entire weekends watching TV and avoiding people. He and his best friends weren't that interested in girls, and they weren't interested in drinking. Forming a band, especially with people he liked, was a splendid way out of his current rut.

With Bono the natural leader aboard, the project gained instant importance. More meetings were planned. Edge's brother Dick and others drifted in and out, but basically the band became the project of Bono, Larry, the Edge, and Adam. The more they got together and talked about the band and made plans, the closer they grew. "Music was very much the secondary thing. We liked each other and got a lot out of it as a social situation," said Adam.

Despite their four distinctly different personalities, they found they often thought alike, shared the same vision, and believed in the same things. Bono found that both Larry and the Edge shared his religious convictions, having a deep faith that found no outlet in traditional Catholicism or Protestantism.

Larry's faith, like Bono's, had been influenced by tragedy. A younger sister died before he'd met his bandmates. Shortly after the band formed, his mother was struck by a truck and killed. This second tragedy served to strengthen his faith: it also brought the four of them closer together.

Though music was taking a backseat to socializing, they were still committed to forming a band and continued trying to put the pieces together.

"We never got into it because we wanted to make a living. It certainly didn't enter my head at that stage," remembered Edge. "I may have been naive but I'm not that stupid."

Larry was happy to be the drummer, but everyone else wanted to be the lead guitarist. Adam switched to bass, and that left Edge and Bono to battle it out for top guitar honors. Edge immediately established himself as an amazingly quick study with incredible musical instincts. Bono soon saw he'd have to settle for rhythm guitar. But even that didn't seem to be his forte. The others weren't quite sure what to do with him. One day they broached the subject of perhaps making him the manager, but Bono drew the line at having to get off the stage entirely. He wasn't a behind-the-scenes type. Why not try singing?

Today Bono is regarded as one of the top vocalists in the world of rock, both in technique and emotional delivery. Little if any of this natural ability was evident when he first tried singing. In fact, he couldn't sing at all. At their next rehearsal, he decided to give it one last try. He opened his mouth, and out came . . . a real voice! "So that's how you do it!" he remembers, thinking to himself. His nickname had proved to be prophetic.

At this point, U2 was a garage band. They cut their teeth on cover songs, trying to learn their instruments copying songs by their favorite bands: Television, Patti Smith, the Rolling Stones. Unfortunately, still not being able to play very well, they weren't able to render renditions that even the most ardent fans of the bands they were copying would be able to identify. There was only one thing to do. If they couldn't fake their way through other bands' songs, they'd have to write their own.

Thus began a period of experimentation and growth. They had absolutely no preconceptions about what they were supposed to sound like, no real outside influences, and proceeded to invent music more than they discovered it.

"Sometimes I have a guilt complex about our roots," said Bono. "We don't have funky black roots. We don't have white rock roots. Our music almost doesn't seem to have roots. It's like totally our own."

With the proper lineup in place and the shackles of imitation abandoned, the essence of the band underwent a dramatic change. Everything suddenly seemed to fit together and make sense. They became much more serious about what they were doing.

By now they had outgrown Larry's kitchen and had taken over a shed in the backyard of Edge's house in Malahide Village for weekend rehearsals. "We wanted something like the power of The Who and something that was as sensitive as Neil Young," remembered Bono, looking back on that formative stage. With each rehearsal, they felt a power growing within them, as though a critical mass was reached and a force unleashed whenever they came together.

"Individually we probably wouldn't have gone anywhere musically," said Adam. "Without any one of us the fragile uniqueness and specialness of U2 would be gone forever."

They were quickly overcoming their technical limitations.

"It suddenly dawned on us that there wasn't such a gulf of musical ability or talent between the stage we were at and the stage that most bands on television and with recording deals were at, so we decided then that we would go for it," Edge remembered.

They developed a sense of mission, though at the time they couldn't quite put their finger on what that mission was. And their commitment seemed to be infectious. The Edge's brother Dick, along with Bono's friend Guggi, started his own group, called the Virgin Prunes, a band that was to have considerable impact on the Dublin music scene and whose beginnings were inextricably linked with U2's.

The growing musical interest of the four was also being noticed at Mount Temple. After the lack of enthusiasm all but Dave Evans showed in their schooling, relief was expressed in certain quarters that there was, indeed, something that piqued the interest of the other three. Here was a chance to put the school's philosophy to the test. Mount Temple had always stood for experimentation, encouraging students to expand the concept of what an education, or a learning experience, is. Although a rock band wasn't exactly what many educators would encourage, some of the teachers thought the boys should be helped. They proposed giving a seldom-used room in one of the outbuildings over to the boys for practice. If, of course, they were serious about what they were doing.

They were.

Now that they had the support of their teachers, school became something they looked forward to. Now nothing could stop them.

The New Wave Breaks

It was 1977. The English punk scene exploded out of London, bringing with it the message that technical competence wasn't nearly as crucial as commitment to what you were doing. Tired old dinosaur groups were threatened with extinction by vital young bands springing up everywhere.

Yet as much as the four were propelled and exhilarated by the message in this movement, they abhorred its proponents—bands who quickly condemned the musical establishment, but were unable to offer an uplifting alternative. That was not the route the four chose for their band. They wanted to make music that was "worthwhile and lasting," that would "transcend any barriers of time and location." As the Edge said, "A lot of pop music is very fixed. It only makes sense if you know what happens to be hip in New York or London that week. I'm sick of music like that."

Or, as Bono put it, "We wanted to separate ourselves from the groups that play 'little music,' which has no heart or soul, no grandness of vision to it, and all sounds very small."

It was time to come up with a name for the band, one that would serve a twofold purpose. First, it would notify people that they were not part of the punk movement, with its snarling, unfocused energy. Second, it would be a name that would be impossible to categorize, so no assumptions could be made about the band.

They tried Feedback, but that didn't wear very well. Neither did the Hype. They don't remember who suggested it, but suddenly the name U2 appeared. That certainly couldn't be easily pigeonholed. Though they were all a bit mystified by it, they agreed that if they wanted a name that wouldn't label them as part of any trend, movement, or sound, U2 was perfect. Deliberately vague, as Bono later said. A name that could conjure up any image you wanted it to, or no image at all.

At this point the band was receiving a good deal of encouragement from the teachers, and fellow classmates were always buzzing about what they were up to in their class/rehearsal room. A history teacher gave them lots of support. Other instruction also played a part. They enrolled in a music course in classical and Renaissance music. Bono claimed this was one of the factors in allowing the band to develop its unique and original sound. Unlike many bands, they weren't overly influenced by blues-based music.

Weekends were still spent in the shed behind Edge's house, where cookies were thoughtfully served by his mother, whom they took to calling Mrs. Edge, just as his father became Mr. Edge. All of their parents, in fact, approved of their musical project.

They were constantly evolving, improving. Although certainly rough around the edges, they had already developed a distinctive style. Larry's drumming, always propulsive and rock-steady, was becoming even more crisp and powerful. The Edge, with his natural affinity for music, was creating a unique approach to guitar playing. Forsaking the heavy power chords favored by most guitarists and almost demanded by a three-instrument lineup, he was developing a more ethereal and evocative style, fashioned out of chiming chords and terse arpeggios floating above Adam's lyrical and imaginative bass. He even credited Adam in a left-handed way for this distinctive sound: "Adam is a very ostentatious sort of person, y'know, very extravagant, so when he started playing bass he wasn't interested in taking the bottom end of the sound spectrum at all. He wanted to be right up there in the mid ranges. . . . In order to give the group any sort of clarity, therefore, I had to stay away from the bottom end of the guitar as much as I could. So I tended to work around those high chords, that ringing sound."

As for Bono—ever the natural showman, it turned out he had a voice to more than match his exuberant manner.

A voice that could find you halfway across a room, pick you up and shake you, and set you back down, forever changed.

They were becoming aware that there was something very powerful in U2. It was more than just commitment— it was a gift. Bono called it a "spark" that set them apart. They viewed their lack of expertise and outside influences as an asset. They were writing new songs all the time, constantly improving, and what was going on in their rehearsal room had a lot more potential than just a school project.

It was time to make their debut. Naturally it would be at Mount Temple. It was early 1978, and their commandeered classroom was packed with schoolmates and teachers. Of course, they were a little nervous, but they had spent months in preparation. Not just learning to play instruments, not just writing songs after finding they couldn't cover other tunes, not just painstakingly trying and discarding a thousand and one musical ideas but, more important, becoming real friends. And together, as friends, believing in what they were doing, they could accomplish anything.

When their forty-five–minute show was over, a mixture of relief, shock, and excitement hung in the air. Relief from teachers who'd championed their cause. Shock over the power and grandeur of their music. And excitement from the four members of U2 themselves. It had spilled from the makeshift stage and swept over every person in the room.

It must have been a great show. Bono said it was two years before another gig sounded as good.

U2 CAN BE A
STAR

*T*hey'd done it. Gone from being a group of friends who couldn't play a note to a real band. Fresh from the success of their first gig, they were eager to play more, just about anytime, anywhere. All they needed was a place to plug in.

At the time, Dublin didn't have a big rock scene. (It still doesn't.) Bands, especially those playing originals, did gigs in pubs and small clubs with names like "Paddy's Punk Party." The few better venues were reserved for the more polished cover bands. As much as they believed in what they were doing, U2 was awed by these technically proficient and established bands.

The pub/club circuit became U2's stage. Never mind that they weren't old enough to drink. They were making good music, customers seemed to like their energy and intensity, and that was all the pub owners cared about.

But while pub owners were willing to look the other way about band members being underage, they weren't so lenient when it came to U2's many young fans. U2 decided to look for a venue where age would be no barrier, but they couldn't find a suitable club.

But who said it had to be a club? Or even in a building? In downtown Dublin was a car park ("parking lot" to Americans), a dirt patch with a low metal roof. Weekdays the lot was filled with commuters' cars. Weekends the lot was virtually empty. Why not play there?

The idea was so crazy it might work. They got permission to use the Gaiety Green car park, built a makeshift stage and blanketed the town with flyers and posters announcing their upcoming series of Saturday performances.

By now word about U2 had spread beyond the classrooms, friends, and families to neighborhood acquaintances and people they'd never met. Those who'd seen them were so enthusiastic that there was a growing crowd of the curious and skeptical. By the time of their first Saturday performance, several hundred people were anxiously waiting.

Anyone who came expecting to see some of the neighborhood kids indulge themselves with a hobby was in for a shock. What they found instead was an incredibly precocious and self-assured unit producing music that managed to be both hard-rocking and inspiringly original. Already they were playing songs that would become future hits: "Trevor," which after many lyric changes became "Touch"; "Silver Lining," which later turned into "11 O'Clock Tick Tock," their first English release; "Stories for Boys"; and "Shadows and Tall Trees."

Others, like "Cartoon World," "The King's New Clothes," and "Concentration Cramp" never made it onto vinyl but still displayed the spark that made their music stand out.

With more confidence in their abilities, the band began to think about long-term prospects and problems. Soon only Larry would be left at Mount Temple, and they'd no longer be able to rehearse in a converted classroom. If U2 was to have a real future, it would have to be handled professionally.

Management Decisions

Adam had essentially inherited the band's management responsibilities. He didn't have that much else to do, since his ceaseless clowning had finally gotten him kicked out of school. He got a job driving a delivery truck but gave it up after smashing in the front end of the vehicle a month later. So he arranged bookings and transportation and handled the finances and was proving himself to be quite the hustler.

But if they were to achieve some of the things they'd dared to talk and dream about since they got together in Larry's kitchen, they'd have to find a professional manager. Someone who could show just as much vision, originality, and sense of dedication to managing the band as they brought to making music, who believed in them as much as they believed in themselves.

Where do you find a manager like that? Are tapes sent to a London management agency? Should you try to get a record deal on the strength of a demo and use the contract as a lure? Should a music industry gadfly be hired? None of these routes was appealing. They wanted someone who would believe in them now, as raw and unpolished as they were. The search began.

There are over half a million people in Dublin, but it's still a small town. The successful citizens are a matter of local pride. Especially the ones who stay there instead of heading for London and its larger slices of fame and fortune. The boys were familiar with one such young and successful Dubliner.

His name was Paul McGuinness, and he had a proven track record as a TV and film producer. He had a string of television commercials to his credit and had been involved with several movies, including *Zardoz* and *The Great Train Robbery*. He was even involved in the Dublin music scene, managing a hot local band called Spud.

They decided McGuinness would be the perfect manager. McGuinness didn't share their enthusiasm. Adam was given the task of trying to recruit him, and thus began several months of begging, pleading, and cajoling just to get McGuinness to agree to come to see them. He began by presenting McGuinness with one of the U2 calling cards they'd had made up even before their first performance at Mount Temple. McGuinness didn't seem very impressed.

It's not surprising he found Adam's invitations so easy to ignore. The town was full of punk bands trying to get by on energy and commitment. He was already having second thoughts about remaining as Spud's manager. Sure, Spud was good, but that didn't seem to matter much in the rock world. This is what McGuinness had been telling Adam for almost the last year. In fact, instead of just declining Adam's invitations, Paul would usually take the opportunity at their brief meetings to encourage him to give up music, even if Adam did go on about how talented and committed the band was. You needed something more.

Yet after months of nagging, as much to put an end to the pestering as out of curiosity, McGuinness went to see U2 play. He certainly had no desire to get involved with them professionally. This was strictly a courtesy call, to once and for all, absolutely, unequivocally, be able to say No!

Soon after McGuinness sat down at a table, the four members of U2 filed onstage. Somehow they didn't look like the same people who'd been after him for a year. Bono made a brief introduction of the group, and they were off.

For the next hour, McGuinness was assaulted by the most urgent, original, and captivating set of rock 'n' roll he'd ever heard. Adam and Larry drove the beat ahead as though controlling a mechanized battering ram. The Edge, with his ringing tones backed by howling feedback, sounded like he was alternately pulling notes from heaven and hell. Yet for all this incredible musical talent and display of force, what really riveted his attention was the lead singer. The one who called himself Bono. McGuinness had seen plenty of singers, but never one with this kind of voice.

As Edge remembered, "I think he did something which not many others did, and that was confront a crowd.... Bono was different. He went out there and he assumed this importance and this character and eyed the audience and was totally impressive."

When McGuinness talked to the band afterward, he realized he'd never paid much attention to what gentlemanly, serious people they were. They weren't like the typical punk musicians that infested Dublin. But it certainly wasn't their manner that ultimately piqued his interest. This was a group that had the "something" that separated the truly inspired and original from the very good. He wasn't interested in drawing up a management contract right away, but he was interested in working with them, seeing whatever he could for them in the near term. As for the long term, well, they'd wait and see.

The boys were ecstatic. Not just that McGuinness agreed to work with them. Far more important was that he believed in them. He'd seen his share of rock groups many times over, and if he picked up on what they thought they saw in themselves ... maybe they weren't crazy after all.

Official manager or not, there were two immediate matters to attend to. Number one, giving McGuinness a nickname. He was christened Magoo. Number two, a request for executive action: get the band a pint at the pub next door—they were still too young to be served!

McGuinness wasn't the only one who felt U2 really had something. They'd never been wallflowers about trying to attract attention, and it was beginning to pay off. Just about everybody who went to see them play came away a believer. Small write-ups about them were starting to appear in the *Hot Press*, Dublin's new rock newspaper, and other local publications.

McGuinness helped the band get work opening for more established Irish bands, but these dates became harder to arrange once groups found out U2 wasn't an easy act to follow.

In the late summer of 1978, they formalized their relationship after much discussion and agreement about their long-term goals and how to go about achieving them. They understood McGuinness didn't have money to invest— what he did have was commitment and business savvy. No one was expecting overnight stardom. They already knew U2 had tremendous potential. But unless it was nurtured properly, they would go nowhere. The key would be constant touring, for U2 came through best in live performance. No matter how good a record they would ever make, this was a live group, one that people would have to see and, having seen once, would want to see and experience again and again. Building a following like this is a slow and steady task not meant for bands whose talents can't support repeated scrutiny by a fickle public whose main interest is in this week's disposable fad.

That's not to say they didn't consider themselves capable of making a good record. They'd been making demos of some of their songs, though all they had was a four-track tape recorder, and they found it couldn't deliver the big sound they were looking for. But they made the most of it, using the equipment's limitations to their advantage by going for a smaller, fragile sound that showed a vulnerability in their music few bands would feel secure enough to reveal.

After they played the tapes for some of their friends, reaction was good enough that they decided to press up a limited number of one song, an early version of "Boy/Girl." Now they were a band with an independent single to their credit.

Ireland's national radio had a midnight rock show hosted

by Dave Fanning. For anyone who cared about what was happening in music, it was the show to listen to. U2 got him a copy of the single, and he liked what he heard. Now they were getting airplay!

Through the fall of '78 they continued working and making demos. Despite the excellent reports from those who'd seen them play, U2 still wasn't considered a real band by many on the scene. They just didn't have the chops of lots of people on the Dublin music circuit, accomplished cover bands. U2 was just a punk group—or so some of these more polished bands thought.

Respected and Dejected

One night in February of 1979, Larry burst into rehearsal. "Have you seen the evening paper? he asked. The paper announced the Guinness and Harp Talent Contest. Sponsored by one of Ireland's largest brewers, it offered £5,000 and a recording contract as first prize for the best unsigned pop band. Adam, Bono, and Edge were skeptical of their chances, but they sent off an entry form anyway.

The contest was scheduled for the day after St. Patrick's Day, in Limerick. The night before, U2 played Dublin's Project Arts Centre. They'd been onstage till three A.M. and managed just four hours' sleep before getting up for the train to Limerick.

When they got to the competition, they found they'd be deprived of their biggest asset—a live crowd. Before making it to the finals, bands had to pass several "heats" by playing without an audience for a panel of judges.

Bono's voice was hoarse and scratchy from his night of singing. "Sorry, I've got laryngitis and my voice is a bit rough," Bono told the judges, "but the songs are good."

They played three songs, and each time they were advanced to the next round. They made it to the last round, now in front of a live audience. They watched the other bands in the competition—show bands, sharp and polished, covering big hits.

"We thought, 'We don't stand a hope,'" remembered Adam. U2 didn't have the flashy stage routine, but they did have that spark, the originality that was instantly recognizable as something very special and unique. Whether or not they won, U2 would give the audience all they had, as they always did. When they finished their brief set, even members of the other bands seemed impressed.

It was time to announce the winners. Awards were presented in reverse order, and the closer they got to announcing the winning band, the more U2 doubted they had any chance for recognition.

"... and number one is ... U2!"

They couldn't believe it! They'd beaten out every top unsigned band in Ireland! As Adam said, "To this very day I can't really figure it out."

One of the prizes was a contract with the Irish arm of CBS records. The £5,000 were a godsend for buying equipment, but they found the promised contract wasn't nearly as useful.

"It was a bullshit contract. We were naive and young, but we still weren't prepared to take it," remembered Adam.

The Irish CBS representative believed in the band, even though he couldn't offer them a better deal, and talked CBS into paying for a demo. They were told to set up as if they were going to do a live show and play a set. Hopefully the recorded results would help land them a proper contract with the company.

"They were awful," Adam later said. "We didn't know it at the time, we had nothing to compare them with. We thought that was the way punk bands got signed. We were giggling and saying, 'Yeah, next week millionaires.'"

The tapes were taken to London, where CBS executives had a good laugh listening. One of them, though, wasn't laughing. A former writer for the rock publication

Sounds, his name was Chas de Whalley. He thought he heard a spark in the raw performances and went up to Dublin to check the band out. Convinced he'd stumbled onto something, De Whalley got CBS to put up the money for a good demo, using himself as producer.

Meanwhile, McGuinness kept U2 on the road. For the first time, they ventured into Northern Ireland for gigs. The four knew about the problems caused by religious differences in the south, but they were unprepared for the amount of bigotry and hatred they saw in the north. They wanted to do something about it. Trying to unite people through their music seemed to be the best way. The response they were now able to generate anywhere in Ireland made them hope that someday they might succeed.

They were building a reputation as one of Ireland's hottest bands. But they were far from being household words. Every night they felt they had to prove themselves all over again.

A typical performance was like one at the Hough Youth Center, outside of Dublin, in August 1979. When U2 had a gig, they let people know. The town would be blanketed with posters announcing the show.

A punk cover band opened the show, grinding out hits by the Ramones, Sham 69, and other favorites. The 250 kids in Hough liked it. Punk was happening.

Then U2 took the stage. They powered through a set of their early hits. "Silver Lining." "The Magic Carpet." "Stories for Boys." An hour of songs; some still famous, others long-forgotten.

It was obvious. U2 was really good. And they were the same age as the kids in the audience. By the end of the set the youth of Hough had been captivated.

After the show, the band came out and talked. They had a tremendous enthusiasm about their music, about meeting people, trying to reach out to them. They signed autographs and answered questions. Bono especially seemed to thrive on this immediate contact.

But despite the enthusiastic response that was becoming standard, once offstage, things were hard for the band. There was never enough money. They cashed in deposits on empty bottles that collected in the dressing room. Yet when Bono was quizzed about these lean times when the band was well on its way to fame and fortune, he'd tell journalists it gave the band endurance. What they really survived on, he said, was their belief that what they were doing was important. At times, belief was all they had.

Even the De Whalley project hadn't gone as they'd hoped. CBS wasn't pleased with the demo and passed on the band. U2 made the best of the situation. They needed a single in Ireland. Why not use the demo? CBS agreed.

In September, their EP *U2 Three* was released by CBS's Irish division. The record has more variations of its spelling than it has songs. On the cover, it's spelled *U2 Three*, but it's also cropped up as *U2-3, U-2-3,* and *U 1-2-3.* Despite any confusion over the spelling, there was none about the content. Featuring "Out of Control," "Stories for Boys," and "Boy/Girl," the disc got immediate attention, and the reviews were favorable. "Out of Control" was picked as the cut to play. Written on the morning of Bono's eighteenth birthday, it was a driving yet wistful paean to the confusion and problems of growing up. The EP made the Irish charts.

To help spread the gospel according to U2, Bono headed to London, with his girlfriend, Alison, in tow, to call on music papers and journalists, and he left those he talked to with tapes of the band and memories of a tremendously loquacious and energetic young man.

Irish rock music was going through a cultural renaissance, left in the wake of the punk explosion. Bands like Radiators from Space, the Undertones, and, in the north, Stiff Little Fingers were creating a stir. U2 was in this category, and everyone around them felt this band was going to be bigger than them all.

The *Hot Press* hadn't been asleep while all this home-grown talent developed. They were big supporters of the growing Dublin scene and decided to publish a readers' poll, asking the public who was best in a variety of categories. The cash prize would help the favorite group buy equipment. When the votes were tallied, it turned out U2 had won in five categories.

Best Group: U2
Best Irish-Based Group: U2
Best Male Singer: Bono
Best Live Band: U2
Best Songwriter: Bono

This made them the top group in Ireland, even if they had no contract.

Despite the local glory, U2 was going through its darkest hour. Larry was the only one left at Mount Temple. As 1980 neared, Bono had already entered and left university, flunking out in part because he had failed Gaelic, owing to his earlier neglect of the subject. The Edge had put off entering college. If he were to go at all, he'd be studying engineering, and the best school for that was far from Dublin. Once he enrolled, the band would be through. It was unthinkable for him to be replaced and impossible for him to continue.

It wasn't the Edge who was keen on engineering school: it was his parents. They'd always supported his involvement with the band, but now they were concerned about his future. Sure, U2 was popular, but what if it wasn't tomorrow? Then what would he do? He'd have no skills!

His parents delivered an ultimatum: If the band didn't have a record contract by the spring term, he'd be packed off to university.

"That was a devastating period of our lives, as you can well imagine," said Edge in retrospect.

Well, if that was the situation, the band wasn't going to sit around moping. There were three months until school would start. In the meantime, they had work to do. First they returned to the studio with Chas De Whalley and recorded a single, "Another Day."

No matter what the future held for U2, one thing was clear: They were getting too big for Ireland. If they really wanted a contract, there was only one place to get one—London!

London Calling

When U2 headed to London in December of 1979, they were Ireland's hottest band. Given the relationship between the Irish and the English, that didn't mean much. Dublin may have had a history of artistic sophistication, but to the typical jaded Londoner, it was the sticks. The unassuming youngsters from Dublin found out why.

While he wouldn't say he was shocked by it, Edge later admitted that the strongest impression the city made on him was of its brazen sexuality. With the conservative approach to dress and advertising promoted by the Catholic Church in Ireland, he found the more liberated attitude of London quite exciting.

Bono, too, was taken aback at the welcome the city offered. He later told reporters of going down into the tube and finding ads filled with underpants and prostitution and people hurrying to get places and things moving incredibly fast.

They didn't have much time to indulge their sense of wonder, with a full schedule of shows booked.

Moonlight Club, West Hampstead; Dec. 1
Nashville, Kensington; Dec. 2
Clapham 101 Club; Dec. 3
Hope and Anchor, Islington; Dec. 4
Rock Garden, Covent Garden; Dec. 5
Electric Ballroom, Camden; Dec. 7, 8

Bridgehouse, Canning Town; Dec. 11
Dingwalls, Camden; Dec. 14
Harrow Road, Windsor Castle; Dec. 15

Their first three nights would be warm-ups, to acclimate them to playing before London audiences. Then the press and record companies would be invited, starting with the gig at the Hope and Anchor in the suburb of Islington. As it was, Edge was playing with his right hand in a cast, thanks to a car accident he'd been in, and despite his prodigious talent they weren't sure he'd be able to play very well. Luckily he was still able to grip the pick and play as brilliantly as ever.

U2's first London tour was met with a yawn. When they hit the Hope and Anchor, only nine paying customers showed up. When Edge left the stage to fix a broken string, the rest of the band followed him, calmly taking up some of the empty seats until it was time to continue.

"I've heard a lot about all your lovely lads and fashions over here," Bono sarcastically told audiences. "Well, U2 aren't either of those."

The following night found them at the Rock Garden in Covent Garden, opening for an up-and-coming all-girl band, the Dolly Mixtures. Before the show began, they heard a writer from *Melody Maker* was in the audience. This could be the break they'd been looking for. They hit the stage and put on a whirlwind performance.

When the next issue of *Melody Maker* hit the stands, the reviewer spent reams of text on the Dolly Mixtures but not a word on U2. Not even their name. That's not to say *Melody Maker* ignored them completely. They were listed in the paper's gig guide for that week—as V2! Naturally the boys let the paper know that wasn't the name of the band, and six days later, when they played the Canning Town Bridgehouse, *Melody Maker* tried to remedy the error. This time they were UR.

But smaller rock journals paid attention. The tapes Bono passed around on his first foray to London had been well received, and reporters and cognoscenti came to check out U2. The underground grapevine by which trendsetters and tastemakers communicated by buzzing about the four lads from Ireland. But it wasn't enough to stimulate the interest of the general public.

The band left London almost as unknown as they'd arrived. Record company interest didn't materialize. Despite the noise their EP had made in Ireland, CBS still wasn't interested. And soon it would be time for Edge to go off to the university.

They returned to Dublin about as demoralized as they had ever been. Weighing their options, they realized, as Adam said, they had two choices: "We either had to break up or do a massive tour." They decided to do the tour.

They would draw strength from the people who believed in them most—fans in cities and towns throughout Ireland. Their EP had done very well, and with "Another Day" set for February release, a tour across the Emerald Isle would generate lots of excitement.

Meanwhile, it appeared their trip to London hadn't been in vain after all. The word of mouth from the few people that had seen them play and the growing buzz from the tapes Bono had given away were starting to have a residual effect. Ecstatic reports were finding their way into print, filed by journalists who had the foresight to see the London dates.

"How many times have you been to see a band for the first time and you know that they have it?" asked *Record Mirror*, in a review of the Rock Garden appearance. "Their confidence, energy and damn good music got to us all. . . . I'll be hearing from them and seeing them again. Unless you keep your eyes and ears closed, so will you. And I bet you get the feeling I'm feeling now."

At *Sounds*, the reaction was even stronger.

". . . The most refreshing new pop music I've heard all year, powerfully pointing along a scintillating guitar sound, a flexible rhythm base and Bono's ever improving, identifying vocals," wrote Dave McCullough. "The effect is, three or four times in 20 minutes, having the hairs on the back of your neck stand on end."

Not everyone saw it that way, though.

"Bono is the archetypal mixed up, fucked up teenager who doesn't know where or how to look for direction," wrote one wag.

With interest percolating in London, *New Musical Express*, often a more adventurous publication than *Melody Maker*, its more venerable competition, decided to dispatch a journalist to cover U2's Irish tour. The ecstatic reports from Limerick, Cork, and other shows were combined into a front-page article that fell all over itself praising the band. It was almost unheard of for an unsigned band to be featured on the cover of *NME*, but an unsigned Irish band? It was without precedent.

Suddenly everybody was talking about U2—especially record companies. And one of the record execs who was most intrigued was Chris Blackwell, the president of Island Records.

Island wasn't big, but it was highly respected, and Blackwell had a reputation of being able to spot emerging trends and up-and-coming talent before most. He had formed Island early in the 1960s to bring reggae music to England, and was credited with introducing the ska and blue beat influence to rock 'n' roll.

Back in '67, Blackwell decided to expand his label's output and promptly turned out hit albums for a number of British rock groups. He brought Traffic, King Crimson, Mott the Hoople, Emerson, Lake & Palmer, Free, and Fairport Convention to the Island roster.

Yet Blackwell wasn't content with financial success. For him, artistic integrity was just as important. As the '70s began, he turned his attention to acquiring bands that, while not commercially viable, were creating trends that many observers felt were musically important. Artists like Roxy Music, John Cale, Brian Eno, Marianne Faithfull, and Suicide.

Blackwell, ever with his ear to the ground, had been

hearing a lot of things about U2, well before *NME* ever thought of dispatching a reporter to check them out. If even a fraction of the stories were true, this was a genuine supergroup in the rough. Now that *NME* had blown the story wide open, he knew every major label in England would be dangling fat contract offers in front of them. It was time to act.

To culminate their Irish tour, U2 booked themselves into the two-thousand-seat National Stadium in Dublin. The show was sold out. No unsigned band had ever been able to book a venue that size in Dublin, let alone pack it.

Blackwell dispatched Bill Stewart, one of his most trusted A&R men, to check the group out.

U2 may have been unsigned, but everything about their performance, about the way they carried themselves, said that they were one of the top rock acts in the world. With their single "Another Day" near the top of the Irish charts, their fans had turned out in force for U2's homecoming show.

Looking out into the adoring audience, Bono said, "Things will not be the same in this city for us." The crowd roared its approval. From the opening chords of "Silver Lining" to the explosive closing with "Out of Control" fifteen songs later, the hall was the scene of love-struck pandemonium. Following the show, Bill Stewart couldn't get to a phone fast enough to deliver a full report to Blackwell.

By now, the band was being besieged with offers from record companies, each promising the world if only they'd sign on the dotted line. But U2 had come too far to give in to the first tempting offer. The band and McGuinness agreed that whoever they signed with would have to give U2 complete artistic control. They would not be rushed into recording or pushed into trying to make hit records instead of good records.

Bono told people he cared about money only for its

ability to buy instruments and to give them a chance to develop. Other than that, they'd done without money for so long that it didn't seem very important.

Idealism sounds great, but in the meantime they had no contract, and Edge's parents were adamant about their ultimatum. He'd registered at the university in January, and with their Irish tour over, he packed away his guitar and set off for engineering school. Even as Bono, Larry, and Adam said good-bye, they felt they'd be meeting again very soon.

PLAYING FOR KEEPS

With Edge away, the others spent their time entertaining recording offers instead of audiences. But contract or not, they wanted to play for the people of London again. They didn't feel they'd gotten a fair shake from the public the first time. The Edge temporarily took leave of his studies for the early March tour.

Things didn't get off to an auspicious start. The evening before they left, a publishing deal that would have earned them some much needed money went awry. For all the talk about the band's wonderful prospects, here they were short on cash and a long way from home, with a key member who couldn't leave his studies every time they called.

No sooner did they start playing in front of London audiences than their concerns disappeared. This time they generated the same response they'd created in Ireland. Now it wasn't a few select critics, record execs and die-hard fans who were paying attention to U2. Everybody was. They returned from their second London tour with a renewed sense of purpose and possibility. This time when they packed Edge off to school, they knew his academic career would be a short one.

Making a Deal

When Chris Blackwell came calling on U2, he didn't
have the sums major labels like CBS and Warner Brothers
could shell out. But he could offer them several things
the majors couldn't or wouldn't—and if his instincts were
right about the band, these would be the most important
considerations.

What Blackwell had to offer was integrity, honesty,
and belief in the band. True, he hadn't been an early
follower, but as far as he was concerned, you only had
to see them once to know they had potential. Blackwell
was willing to let that potential be realized at its own pace.
Where the other companies were talking about a willing-
ness to invest money, Blackwell was willing to invest time.

He'd give them the artistic freedom and control he
knew a band like U2 needed. Companies that offered fat
advances pressured bands into churning out "big-selling
albums" and "hits," to recoup their investment. That's
not what Blackwell was looking for.

"A lot of people came with money," Bono recalled.
"Island was the only one that talked in terms of music."

Back from London, U2 were ready to make a decision
about their recording future. The tremendous British response had gone a long way toward sweetening offers
from some companies and induced others to make initial
bids. But as they toted up the cash and benefits dangled
in front of them, they kept coming back to one important
consideration: What mattered most was artistic control.
Money was only a secondary part of the contract.

"The sticking point was always whether they'd let us
deliver the records without any opportunity to refuse them
and there are large companies that just can't handle that,
the whole corporation has a hiccough," observed Mc-
Guinness. "They imagine the worst."

* * *

U2 signed with Island Records in April 1980, and the
Edge checked out of engineering school for the last time.
With their financial worries over and artistic control as-
sured, they headed for the studio. Producing was Martin
Hannett, who'd worked with Magazine, poet John Cooper
Clarke, and Joy Division, the English band noted for its
stark musical conceptions and fragile sensitivity.

After laying down several tracks, the band picked "11
O'Clock Tick Tock," which evolved from "Silver Lining,"
to be released in May as their first single.

With its fat opening guitar chordings and schizophrenic
structure, it was a great record. But at four-and-a-half
minutes, it was about two minutes too long to have any
hope of getting on the tightly controlled BBC, England's
government radio, a network with a virtual monopoly on
the ears of English radio listeners.

"We want to beat the music business at its own game
by being successful and important within the industry
without sacrificing one ounce of our integrity or our honesty by doing it our way," Edge explained.

When journalists questioned Bono about Island's will-
ingness to release a single like that from a band that created such high expectations, his explanation: "People there
really believe in the group. They never wanted us to be
a pop group."

The critical reaction was extremely positive to the single, though a bit muted. Many skeptics were waiting for
a complete album before going out on a limb for the band.
Those who said it was too long to get on the radio were
right. As a result of lack of exposure, the single never
made the charts outside of Ireland.

U2 wasn't greatly disturbed by not cracking the English charts on their first try. They had willingly chosen
a difficult path toward their goals, but it was the one they
believed was right. If it took longer to do it their way, so
be it.

Yet as pleased as they were with the single, they didn't

feel Hannett was the right man to handle production of their first album. He was a bit too trendy in his tastes for U2 and preferred a grittier, more muted sound that had become his trademark. "Hannett brought Hannett's sound and it was a struggle to make it U2's," said Bono.

They were anxious to get back in the studio and start working on their first album. But until they could find the right producer, any recording would have to be put on hold.

The band went on tour. With "11 O'Clock Tick Tock" in the shops, they hit the U.K., giving people all over the British Isles their first look at U2, now being called the Next Big Thing.

In the spring and summer of 1980, it seemed as if U2 played at every club, pub, and minor rock venue in the country. Word of mouth was growing every day. For the band each show was a new test, every set played as though it were their first and last. In Birmingham, they drove themselves into such a frenzy that Edge and Adam joined Bono when he leapt off the stage into the audience. Unfortunately, the guitar cords came unplugged, leaving Bono and Larry to play as a duo for several bars.

Even *Melody Maker* was jumping on the bandwagon. In July of 1980 they ran a breathless account of U2's concert at Clarendon Hotel in London, with words like "passion," "honesty," "commitment," and "humility." These adjectives were getting a workout from every rock journalist who contributed a line of ink to U2's growing pile of enthusiastic write-ups. The show ended with Bono handing the microphone to the exhausted audience. To sum it up, the review ended, "easily the finest display of awe-inspiring rock that I've witnessed in a long time. It contained just about every emotion that rock attempted to evoke—from anger to savagery, beauty, and that indefinable essence where words become useless."

But the critics were still a little unfamiliar with the songs. This particular one misidentified the band's closing number, "Electric Company," as "Electric Opening," as

Bono's Irish vocal gyrations got a bit lost in translation.

With the tremendous response to their shows bolstering their confidence, U2 was thinking more and more about their debut album. Already some cynics were starting to ask if there was ever going to be a first album. Perhaps most discouraging, many who asked these pointed questions had once been U2's biggest champions.

Three things to understand about the English music press: 1, They're very powerful. 2, They're very fickle. 3, They can be quick to disown talent they initially spot.

While most of the popular music press was just picking up on U2, some critics had been hailing the band for two years. And now that U2 was becoming phenomenally popular, a few of these early supporters were uncomfortable extolling the band's virtues. They felt it wasn't chic to like a band that was no longer the secret of a few dedicated tastemakers. Some were saying there was little to show for those two years other than stirring live performances, two singles, and an EP which hadn't penetrated the English charts.

Many bands in U2's position, other critics argued, would be working on their second album by now. What was holding up U2? Given the long wait for their first album, some felt it was bound to be a disappointment no matter what they put out.

Yes, it was time for an album. Not because the English pop press demanded one, but because U2 was ready to make one. They'd been held up searching for the right producer. Now it looked like they'd found him. Already breaks from their English tour were being spent at Dublin's Windmill Lane Studios, and the band was very enthusiastic about what was happening there.

Going for the Record

U2 didn't want a "formula" producer, someone known
for a set way of doing things.

They had developed an experimental studio style from
the time of their first four-track demos to their EP and
singles, and they wanted to pursue it on their first album.
Many bands and producers go into the studio knowing
what they're going to do, with a minimum of improvisa-
tion. (Not surprising, given the hourly rates for studio
time.) U2 liked to approach recording the opposite way.
They needed somebody who was not only a technical
expert but who was also willing to stake his reputation
on U2's belief in themselves. If the finished album was
judged a study in self-indulgence, the producer would be
in for more than his fair share of blame.

There was no shortage of people who'd be dying to
burst the bubble of the Next Big Thing. Whoever produced the album would be on the line as much as U2.
How many top-level producers would be willing to give
in to U2's improvisatory recording habits on such an important debut?

At least one. Steve Lillywhite came to the project the
long way around. When U2 sought him out, Lillywhite
had already worked for Island as a staff producer but left
when he felt the label wasn't getting him enough work.
Whatever his relations with Blackwell had been in the
past, the U2 project was important enough to bring him
back.

Steve Lillywhite was born into a musical family in
Egham, outside of London. Both his parents played instruments, and his younger brother was an accomplished
drummer who had gone on to join the respected London-
based Members. Steve himself "fiddled about," as he put

it, on guitar, piano, and bass, and played in several bands in school as he grew up. But he showed a much greater interest in the technical side of music making.

A friend of his worked at Phonogram's Marble Arch Studios in London, and one day Steve dropped around to see him. The day he showed up, someone got fired. Lillywhite got the job on the spot.

"I bluffed my way into it by pretending I had all the right qualifications," he later admitted. He was seventeen years old.

He spent four-and-a-half years at the Marble Arch Studios, getting a thorough apprenticeship in every aspect of recording. He went from glorified gofer to the house engineer.

There was a tremendous fringe benefit: Lillywhite had access to the studios, if not booked, on the weekends for personal recording projects. He made the most of the opportunity, producing demos for a number of struggling bands. One of them was his younger brother's group, the Members. Another was a popular band called Ultravox, and the demo he produced for them led to a deal with Island. The band wanted Lillywhite to produce the album, but Island wasn't keen on turning the project over to an untested producer. But Ultravox was adamant, so Island reached a compromise. They named Lillywhite coproducer, with a seasoned pro overseeing the recording. Island came up with an unexpected choice: Brian Eno, who was himself to play a part in the U2 story some years down the road.

The album, however, was mercilessly panned. Lillywhite might have been discouraged, but Island was impressed with his work; so impressed they offered him an ambiguous job on their production staff.

On Lillywhite's first day, he learned the person who hired him had left the company the previous week. No one knew what Lillywhite was supposed to do. Instead of waiting for them to notice he was unnecessary, he created his own niche, and eventually wound up producing Eddie and the Hot Rods, Steel Pulse, and Ultravox's second album.

Chris Blackwell noticed Lillywhite's board work, knowing that talented producers are as rare as talented musicians; perhaps more so. Blackwell kicked him upstairs and gave him a producer's contract through the label's management arm, Island Artists. Lillywhite got a yearly advance against royalties from any albums he produced, and could still work independently with any non-Island artist he wanted.

That was in 1977. The punk explosion was rocking London with full force. Lillywhite became a fixture on the club scene, meeting bands by night and recording them by day. He produced a string of hit records for local bands, but when he stopped to examine his track record, he saw none of the hits were for Island Records. Perhaps Island wasn't looking out for his future as well as he'd like. At the very least, they weren't giving him a chance to work with the label's top bands.

After talking it over with Blackwell, they agreed to terminate his production contract. Since then he'd been a successful, full-time independent producer, working with the Psychedelic Furs, XTC, the Thompson Twins, Toyah, and Penetration, among others, and now was considered the hottest young producer in England.

Lillywhite was in Dublin to see a show of Tom Robinson's, whom he'd recorded. Waiting for him backstage was a note. "Could Steve Lillywhite please contact Adam Clayton from U2."

Lillywhite had certainly heard of the band but at first didn't even bother responding to the note. Eventually, though, he went back to Ireland to see them play after they'd signed to Island, and was immediately hooked.

"They were so young. I'd always been the youngest— and I was producing at quite an early age, 23 or so—and for the first time there was this band and I was five years older than the eldest guy."

Lillywhite had just finished producing Peter Gabriel's third solo album. Gabriel was about as seasoned a studio recording artist as there is. It would be interesting and challenging to work with a group at the opposite end of the spectrum.

U2 and Lillywhite started work at Dublin's Windmill Lane Studio in July 1980. Almost immediately everyone realized magic was being released in the low gray building set off in Dublin's decaying industrial hub. Lillywhite's production style turned out to be exactly what U2 was looking for, and the collaboration unleashed an avalanche of creativity.

"Steve Lillywhite brought us the brains of the technology to get what we wanted out of the studio. Steve was an open enough personality to tell us how to do what we wanted," said Bono.

The first song they recorded together was "A Day without Me," and based on the strength of that collaboration, Lillywhite was asked to do the album. U2 was so impressed with the song that they decided to put it out as a single, even before the album was finished. It was hardly the up-sounding record most bands were making. Bono wrote the song partly in reaction to hearing that Ian Curtis of Joy Division (the band their earlier producer Martin Hannett had worked with) had committed suicide.

So naturally did Lillywhite's production style fit the band that Adam said, "I'm sure if he wasn't producing us he'd probably be a member of the band anyway."

To anyone who asked, Lillywhite was quite straightforward in saying he'd never enjoyed working with a band as much as he did with U2, a band with such creativity and imagination.

"Everyone was in such a good frame of mind," Lillywhite later remarked about the project, "ideas would just flow."

The recording of "I Will Follow," written three weeks before they entered the studio, was particularly inspired.

"I had a bicycle turned upside down; Bono and I would

spin the wheels and hit the spokes with a knife. There were also bottles smashing all over the place. We were having a great time—just like little kids."

"A Day without Me" was released in August, and again the record was well received by the press and their fans. But the BBC, and the record-buying public in general, still ignored them. The record failed to chart in England. U2 hardly had time to care. They continued their exhausting tour schedule, using their infrequent days off the road to duck into Windmill Lane for more work on their album.

They rerecorded some of the songs they'd originally released on their Irish EP as well as singles, including "Out of Control" and "Stories for Boys." This time they got the sound they were looking for. The band had over forty songs in their repertoire, and one of the hardest parts about making the album was deciding which of the tunes not to record.

Each time they left the studio and went back on the road, they were more confident about how the record was going, and it spilled over into their live performances. By September *Melody Maker* was willing to go out on a limb and say, "U2 should establish themselves as one of the best things to come out of Ireland since James Joyce and Guinness."

Journalists made the pilgrimage north to Windmill Lane with the eager sense of responsibility with which the faithful set off for Mecca. They found U2 in a high state of excitement, scarcely able to control their enthusiasm for the work in progress. Whenever anyone would ask about the band, Bono would explain that U2 was really the story of four friends, not a band. As he made clear to *Melody Maker*'s reporters, U2 was "four people, four individuals, four friends" before they were a band, and it had been that way ever since.

Meanwhile, people were still trying to pigeonhole U2 and their explosive brand of music into an easily identifiable category. They weren't a punk band or "new romantics" with the Edge's heavy use of reverb and feedback, maybe they were "neopsychedelic."

"People have been trying to put their finger on us for a long time.... Why won't they accept us for being four people?" asked Bono.

In September they returned to London for more dates, now in prestigious venues like the Marquee and the Lyceum. They were teamed with Echo and the Bunnymen for some of the shows. The Bunnymen were considered the leading proponents of the neopsychedelic movement, which promoters felt made this an inspired double bill. It's doubtful the Bunnymen felt that way after they were blown off the stage by U2 at every show they played together.

By now the album was done, and as they listened back to the first test pressings, U2 was almost frightened of what they'd unleashed. Either they were crazy, or they had created one of the best debut albums of the last ten years. From the insistent guitar line that opened "I Will Follow" to the fade-out on the surrealistic "Shadows and Tall Trees" that ended it, the album demanded that people sit up and pay attention.

Boy, Bono later said, was something of an autobiographical album; it was about love and sex and their relationship to growing up. The big hit "I Will Follow," despite its raucous rock beat, was practically a lament, a protest song against the inevitable maturing from the comforting and secure world of childhood to the stark world of adults.

The second song, "Twilight," was, according to Bono, the story of "a boy...being confronted by a man who was a homosexual." Certainly that puts the ambiguous lyric of "In the shadow, boy meets man" in a much more highly charged context.

As in most U2 songs, there's much more than one interpretation or intended meaning. For Bono also meant the song to be about menopause and about the problems of aging in general.

"I can remember being told in school about the change in life and how distressing it can be for old men when they stop functioning. I can remember my nervous laugh."

"An Cat Dubh" was about the cat as a symbol of temptation and even evil.

"At first beautiful, you know, seductive. In the daylight it destroys a birdnest. Not for food but for enjoyment and at the same time it comes up to you and strokes the side of your leg," Bono explained.

The second side opened with "Stories for Boys." It's about a child first realizing that life isn't as exciting in everyday life as it is in adventure magazines. Bono believed the effect of this discovery is disillusion, and feeling that you're not worthwhile unless you can turn life into an adventure fantasy. U2 stood for the ability of each individual to make his or her life meaningful, an "adventure."

"The Electric Co." was about a friend of Bono's who'd been committed to a Dublin mental health institution and subjected to electroconvulsive therapy. Bono went to visit him in the institution.

"He told me there's only two ways out of the place— either over the wall or just cut his throat. . . . I feel like there's a high level of mental illness in this country. And I think there's a link between that and a kind of spiritual unrest."

U2 had deliberately moved away from a conventional-sounding record, and that extended all the way to the album cover, which they designed themselves. It was an assembly of four black-and-white head shots that had been processed to keep the features deliberately vague. As far as U2 was concerned, they, as individuals, were unimportant. Anything you needed to know about them was there in the music.

Shortly before *Boy* was relesed, McGuinness received a letter from the A&R department of Warner Brothers, the label that distributed Island's records in the United States. McGuinness had sent a demo tape to Warner's prior to their signing with Island, and now, in a belated reply, Warner's informed McGuinness they were passing on the band.

McGuinness quickly fired off his own reply.

"I thought they might like to know they were releasing our album in a few weeks."

IT'S A BOY!

*I*n October of 1980, U2's debut album, *Boy*, was released in England. Saying the response was positive is one of the great understatements in rock history. *Melody Maker*'s verdict: "U2's live performances have raised their audience's expectations to what must have seemed like an impossible height, but not only have they reached that peak with their first album, they've risen above it."

Critics were ranking *Boy* alongside the top debut albums of all time—Patti Smith, Roxy Music, the Velvet Underground. Some even said U2's album left all those others far behind.

They chose "I Will Follow" as the single, but they were surprised that initially the jacket got more attention than the record. Seeking to avoid creating a cult of personality, they had decided to leave their pictures off the sleeve entirely. Instead, the jacket pictured a neighborhood youth from Dublin shown shirtless from the waist up.

There were whispers that they and the photographer, Hugo McGuinness, were promoting child pornography. For the American single release, they changed the cover art "to stop any concern about pedophilia and the like," as Bono put it.

The story of the boy, and how he became their symbol,

dispells any notions about kiddie porn. The boy's first appearance on a U2 product had been a full year earlier, when he graced the cover of the *U2 Three* EP. Bono explained that "he happens to be a kid who lives across the street from me. We put him on the cover because he's a pretty smart kid. And sometimes I wonder what his future will be like—and I wonder about ours."

But he wasn't just "a kid who lives across the street." He was the younger brother of Bono's childhood pal Guggi, and his real name is Peter Rowan. Being a next generation Lyptonian, he too has a nickname: Radar.

The innocence, intelligence, and sensitivity that Radar represented to the band became the image by which the band presented itself to the world. They had a backdrop made with a large blown-up picture of Radar and began using it as their symbol onstage.

If people wanted to call that kiddie porn, let them. U2 had work to do. They hit the road for a major tour of England to support the album.

Now it wasn't the Next Big Thing as far as the press and tastemakers were concerned; it was the Big Thing. The four good friends from Ireland were subjected to incredible pressure, including the predictable complaints that all the press ravings were nothing more than hype. Bono's response?

"I don't feel we have been hyped by the music press because I happen to agree with the good things they say about us."

He certainly had no fear that U2 would wilt under public scrutiny: "It is a pressure, but if people come along expecting the world from U2, then they're gonna get it. I'm not scared that we won't be able to give it to them."

They'd begin with "The Ocean." Bono would shout at the audience, "Forget about what you've read about us—make up your own minds!" Then the band would launch into a furious version of "11 O'Clock Tick Tock," and the floor would shake.

Yet this was no time for overconfidence. "By no means,

at this point, have we cracked England," commented Adam.

Cracked or not, they took England by storm, and following the tour, Adam was willing to sound a bit more optimistic.

"In England we've done surprisingly well. They know about us, they've heard our records, they've seen our pictures, and they want to know more."

London calls the beat that Europe dances to. When U2 had that city buzzing, European rock capitals picked up on it. Their records had been available as imports in some of the specialty record shops. Now with the album and single getting great critical response, it was time to move beyond England.

It was part of the plan to expand U2's reach, along with their own vision and abilities. U2, they felt, was more than a band. It was a feeling, a force, that could give something to each person it touched. And the more people it touched, the greater the force would grow.

"Some have said that U2 music is for the head and feet," Bono commented as they prepared to leave for the Continent, "but I think it's for the heart as well."

They embarked across the Channel for a tour of Belgium and Holland. The Dutch were well informed musically, if not culturally. Bono found the crowd at the Milky Way, where they played, to be "seriously in the sixties." "Junkies just hanging around . . . a very sick sight."

Despite the constant work, they kept the creative juices flowing. McGuinness, in particular, was astounded to witness them write a song on the spot in Holland. "This roadie handed the Edge a guitar that was supposed to be in tune, but was actually in a different tuning than usual even though it was still harmonious. Edge struck the guitar. Once. I immediately stopped the band and asked Larry to play a beat, and we just went into it. The tape recorder was rolling, and five minutes later there was a song with verse, chorus, lyrics, theme, everything. It was called, 'Be There.'"

But U2 was still basically an underground band in Europe. They played clubs and halls one hearty journalist willing to accompany them called "small and seedy." Naturally U2 did everything they could to bridge the barriers of language and culture.

"Every night is a struggle to communicate," Bono said.

The struggle was taking its toll. By the time the tour neared its conclusion at Appledoorne, in Holland, the cold wet season had come close to making even the stoic Bono sick.

At the final performance at Brussel's Klacik Club, Bono was practically flat on his back from the flu, only finding the strength to stand when "Show time!" was announced.

The tour was a success, but it was hard to tell how genuine the response was. The crowds had been enthusiastic, the venues full, but they weren't sure if the display of affection was for U2 or was just because they were simply a band from the other side of the Channel.

They certainly never thought of themselves as an English band and felt a twofold estrangement from all that those groups represented. They were outsiders by birth and choice. In the first case, the English traditionally look upon the Irish with disdain. In the second, U2 had no desire to be identified with the English music scene and the supposedly hip music it produced.

"Contemporary bands sell their emotions on pieces of plastic at supermarkets and then bend their emotions to suit a market," opined Bono.

U2 would really find their talents tested soon, however—an East Coast tour of the United States would take place in December. They would play only small clubs, but even then they weren't bashful about telling journalists where they really thought they ought to be playing, as one reported after catching up with them in Europe.

"U2 have an unswerving faith that they have the right to the Madison Square Gardens and the saturation of the airwaves that success will bring eventually and while that sounds more than a little immodest, a little naive to others, the sentiments do strike a chord with those who have sampled the character and the sturdiness of their chosen type of musical expression."

Their return from Holland was not entirely joyous. Neither their acclaimed debut album nor their single had made it onto the English charts. Again it was the government–controlled radio holding up the works.* You could have critics doing front-page stories on you every day, and it didn't make a difference unless you could be heard on the radio. They saw radio as a key to success.

For now, there was little they could do about it. At least not in England. Things were a little different in the United States.

The American Plan

Preparations for their American conquest had begun some months before. U2 has often been called a "thinking person's band," but they've earned this distinction for what they do not just onstage but offstage, too. They'd carefully studied the ways and whys of the music business in the United States and found a chink in the armor that kept new bands off the air.

America, they found, had its own version of the BBC. It was called AOR. Not a government controlled network, AOR stood for "Album-Oriented Rock," a tightly regimented format that left little room for playing anything besides the biggest-selling, often least-inventive, groups. AOR was the most popular radio format in the United States. The top rock station in any city was most likely

---

*The BBC was too conservative to play anything remotely connected to the Punk phenomenon, the movement born with angry, antiestablishment songs like "Anarchy in the U.K." and "God Save the Queen," which programmers and other officials regarded as a slap in the face.

following the format. The Eagles. Linda Ronstadt. The Doobie Brothers. Styx. This was AOR. Some of these stations had less desire to play new, unproven records than the BBC did.

There were some sympathetic programmers at these big AOR stations, but what could they do? They couldn't play music people didn't want to hear. Sure, these programmers had heard about the excitement coming out of England with all the New Wave bands, but they weren't about to put the Sex Pistols on their turntables. That was just too raw, too new, too . . . dangerous! They'd stick with California stadium rock for the time being and hope that some New Wave band would come along that had the energy of these punk and New Wave groups, yet sounded great.

U2, however, discovered there was growing disenchantment with the stranglehold the AOR formats held on the radio, and a number of alternative outlets were rapidly developing. There were about thirty-five stations across the country playing what was being called new music, and they were quickly becoming influential. Stations like WBCN in Boston, WLIR in New York, KROQ in Los Angeles, and WXRT in Chicago would play import records or add something daring to a playlist. They were determined to expose the American radio audiences to the overseas sound.

In addition to these major commercial radio stations, there were over two hundred college stations that played the most obscure and avant-garde records. This is where English bands were being heard in the United States.

There was even an alternative to the *Billboard* record chart ratings that had dominated the industry for years. Put out by the *College Media Journal,* or *CMJ,* these charts carried weekly reports on the hottest New Wave and import records, which commercial and college radio stations were playing them, and how often. The whole alternative radio scene was having a growing impact on the American music industry.

U2 realized that these stations would play a part in conquering the United States.

But they couldn't depend on radio alone. Dance clubs were also taking a pivotal role in introducing American audiences to English groups. The clubs were always hungry for new bands and new records. Getting copies of these discs wasn't easy. Clubs in New York or Los Angeles or San Francisco might have access to a specialty record store that handled imports, but what about the clubs spread across the smaller towns of America?

Some enterprising dance-club DJs in New York established a service called Rockpool in 1979. Its purpose: to provide dance club subscribers with a monthly packet of the latest import singles from England and a tip sheet telling which were the hottest. Rockpool was having a difficult time making a go of it in the early days. Record companies could see little reason to give away fifty or a hundred records of their acts for the sake of exposure on American dance floors.

Not everyone was so myopic about the benefits of dance-floor exposure. Among the first to see the possibilities: U2.

One of Rockpool's earliest supporters and boosters was Paul McGuinness. As soon as "11 O'Clock Tick Tock" had been released in England, he sent a couple of bags full of records over, and it became one of the first import records Rockpool serviced to dance clubs. It didn't get great response on the floors, not being the greatest of dance records, but it made an impression.

When "A Day without Me" was released as a single in England, again McGuinness had a batch of the discs shipped to Rockpool. This time the reception was a little warmer.

McGuinness also burned up the transatlantic phone lines, filled with questions about what was being played on the radio, what was making it on the dance floor, gathering every scrap of information he could. He concluded that by the end of 1980, U2 would be ready for

America, and America might just be ready for U2. But the band couldn't depend only on allies at dance clubs and a few alternative radio stations.

To get work, a band needs a booking agency. The better the agency, the better the gigs. There are hundreds of bookers across the country, and the biggest and most prestigious of all is Premier Talent.

Headquartered in New York City, Premier deals only with the world's top rock acts. Certainly U2 considered themselves in this category, but there weren't hordes of top music execs who would agree at this stage in the band's career. This made it somewhat unusual that Paul McGuinness found himself with an appointment to meet with Frank Barselona, the president of Premier Talent, one afternoon in the fall of 1980.

McGuinness wanted Premier to be the band's booking agent in the United States. He didn't want Premier's clout to book the band into the biggest venues they could find. U2 thrived on the personal contact that can be established only by playing in small clubs. They wanted to start out in the United States just as they had in Ireland, and then in England, reaching out to people on a grass-roots level. That meant the agency's commission for making the bookings might not be very lucrative to begin with, but McGuinness believed in the band as he'd never believed in anything before, and he knew that Premier wouldn't regret signing them.

Frank Barselona had heard the talk about the Next Big Thing many times in the past, and nine out of ten bands that were stuck with that albatross of a reputation were never heard from again. He'd also met his share of managers who talked a big game and professed to believe in their bands. But Barselona had never met a manager like McGuinness. He hadn't spent a lifetime in the music business, and was amazingly forthright, intelligent, and sincere. The kind of man you'd want for a friend, whose word was gold. Barselona agreed on the spot to represent U2.

Things were falling into place. U2 had now established contacts with the people who controlled dance floors across the country. They had identified the key radio stations that would help them get airplay. And now they had the clout of the world's top booking agency behind them. All that was left was to put U2 in front of an American audience.

U2 arrived in the United States in December of 1980. This was to be a reconnaissance mission, not a full-scale assault.

They were booked into a few clubs along the East Coast, to give them a chance to meet people and get comfortable in front of American audiences.

There was nothing unusual about such a foray. Sir Freddy Laker's cut-rate transatlantic flights made it rather routine for new English bands to hop over, play a few dates, and go back home where they could book themselves as just returned from a smash U.S. tour.

Whatever they expected, U2 was unprepared for the exuberance and vitality they found in the streets of New York, their first stop. It was almost too intimidating, even for people as self-assured as they were. And their first public appearance took them out of the frying pan and directly into the fire.

The Mudd Club was the most happening club in New York. Tucked away into one of the seedier downtown neighborhoods in New York, its very name chosen as an affront to its ultrachic clientele, the likes of which had included Princess Caroline and virtually every other young jet-setter who wanted to go slumming among the punks and poseurs who ruled Manhattan's nightlife.

U2 chose this club for its American debut. Danny Heaps, the club's DJ, with a reputation as one of the most astute platter spinners in Manhattan, had gone out of his way to land U2's first American booking, promising them $500, even though he knew it was unlikely they'd pull in that much business. Even if the club lost money, it would be a booking he could be proud of for many years.

The club was far from packed, but many of what would be called the right people were there. Several things had attracted them to the club on Thursday, December 11, three days after John Lennon had been killed. The ecstatic reviews and attention had seeped across the Atlantic, and the crowd wanted to know what all the fuss was about. The import single of "I Will Follow" was getting heavy dance club play. Others were drawn by the stamp of approval given by Premier Talent in signing the band, despite the fact that their record had yet to be released in the United States.

The band, keyed up at being in the United States, put on a blistering show. One observer remembering the show asks rhetorically, "They don't do drugs, do they? Cause I remember Bono, he was wild! He came offstage and he was pounding on doors, screaming!"

Another curious observer that night was Joel Webber, an independent record promoter, lured down by the buzz that was beginning to develop Stateside about the band. His verdict? "I saw them and said, 'Jeez, they're going to be huge!'"

After New York, the band went to Boston, then down to Washington where they opened a show for the Dickie Boys, a local favorite.

At this point U2 wasn't blowing anybody off the stage. American audiences didn't know what to make of these energetic and committed youngsters. There was no denying the power and urgency of the music, but American crowds were going to need a little more indoctrination before U2's magic would cast its spell.

Their last U.S. show was back in New York, at the Ritz, the city's biggest and most popular rock dance club. Word of mouth was building on the band, but not enough to fill the two-thousand-seat club.

While the performance was good, it wasn't one of the nights of magic they would be able to reproduce almost routinely on their next swing through the States. Yet, looking back on their minitour as they flew to Ireland, they agreed it had been a success. They'd been able to call on radio stations and DJs, gotten a feel for American audiences, and paved the way for a return visit.

By February, U2 was back on the road in England. That month readers of *New Musical Express* voted them the Best New Act of the year. But despite all the lavish praise, *Boy* and "I Will Follow" had yet to crack the English charts.

Yet one would think they were the biggest-selling band ever to play the British Isles, based on the overwhelming demand for tickets and the incredible response that greeted them on this tour.

It was on this tour that *Rolling Stone*'s James Henke first met up with them. Realizing something important was happening, *Rolling Stone* had dispatched their man to see what all the fuss was about. Bono was more than happy to tell him.

"I don't mean to sound arrogant," he announced, "but even at this stage I do feel we are meant to be one of the great groups."

Henke didn't quite know what to make of Bono and his three friends. The boys took him along to have a bite to eat at a Greek restaurant one evening before a show, and Bono put on an impromptu performance, dancing while patrons smashed plates against the floor to the accompaniment of a bewildered bouzouki player.

By now the buzz about U2 had grown into a roar reverberating across the United Kingdom. Here was a group with no chart action, yet they had no trouble packing the most prestigious venues wherever they played. Rather than wilt under the demands of greatness, they thrived.

The English tour concluded with a show at London's Lyceum, with the Thompson Twins in support. The show had sold out as soon as it was announced, but even those with no chance of getting in couldn't keep away. While the crowd inside the Lyceum held a riotous reunion with

the band from Ireland, another seven hundred stood outside, unable to get tickets but unwilling to miss the event
entirely.

Europe was next on the agenda. Starting on February
9, 1981, in Stockholm, they conducted a whirlwind assault
of the Continental capitals—twelve shows in thirteen
days—in venues like the Paradiso in Amsterdam, Berlin's
Kantkino, and le Palace in Paris. But not all the audiences
were receptive to U2's message. When they played Onkel
Poe's in Hamburg on the fifteenth, the crowd's lack of
enthusiasm led Bono to deliver his now-famous chastise-
ment, "In my country, it's customary to applaud when
the song's over."

They couldn't really be too disappointed. It was only
their second trip to Europe. They'd had to travel back
and forth across England many times before audiences
responded to them, and there they even spoke the same
language.

With Europe and England out of the way, it was time
to turn their attention back to the United States, where
Boy was about to be released.

"It is my intention to travel to America," Bono announced, "and give it what I consider it wants and needs."

BACK IN THE U.S.A.

*I*n March of 1981 *Boy* was released in the United States, and U2 returned to support it. Interest had been building in their absence, fueled by "I Will Follow" as well as reports from the shows during their December visit.

In retrospect, their brief sojourn Stateside had been a masterstroke of strategic planning. They'd given America just enough to leave them hungry for more. People along the East Coast were used to seeing the top new bands, but groups rarely held up as well live as they did on the records that preceded them. The word on U2 was different. If anything, the three import singles didn't do justice to the power the band was able to create in concert. Few could put their finger on what it was that made U2 so important, yet everyone treated the proposition as an undeniable fact.

Maybe it wasn't all because of the band. Maybe part of it was that people were fed up with what passed for popular music, the slick, homogenized glop dominating the airwaves. They'd been waiting literally years for the New Wave explosion to fulfill its promise and deliver an acceptable alternative to the music-as-usual that numbed the mind as well as the spirit. There must be someone to prove that there was a better way, a group who could point to the true path of rock 'n' roll righteousness. It seemed U2 might be that band.

Their first stop was the Ritz, where they'd ended their last American tour. But other than location there were few similarities between that gig and this one.

Ben Manilla, the top-rated jock on Long Island's progressive WLIR, doubled as the Ritz's weekend MC and had seen all manner of crowds at the club.

"I never saw the place as packed as it was that night. ...There was an incredible buzz about the band," he remembered.

The Ritz is not an easy venue to play. It's cavernous and echoey, and even the best of bands have trouble mastering its troublesome acoustics. It also tends to attract a record industry–oriented crowd, ready to pass judgment and dismiss the latest hot band. Certainly these doubters were out in force along with the hundreds who were ready to believe U2 represented something new, vital, and important.

The band fired its opening salvo with "11 O'Clock Tick Tock." Despite his confidence, which sometimes borders on cockiness, even Bono was a bit unnerved by the size and unspoken expectations of the crowd.

There was no stage show—no theatrics, no fancy lights. But there was something much more important. An unbearably complex yet simple sound that filled every corner of the packed club. Yet this was not the outgoing, brash group that had stormed up and down the British Isles for the past year and a half. The band huddled together onstage, almost afraid of the impact they were making, or perhaps worried it would dissipate if they didn't stick together

As they worked their way through the set, Bono became more comfortable with the riotous reception and took control of the crowd. He plunged into his usual expansive performance, patrolling the stage, playing to the balcony, touching the people jammed up against the front of the proscenium. This was the kind of magic that had eluded them on their last visit. Now U2 was ready for America.

By the end of the show, everyone in the audience realized they had witnessed an event, not a concert. What they saw and heard went way beyond music. As Manilla put it, "I don't think there was a doubt in anybody's mind when they left there that they'd seen something very special. U2 had it, they really had it."

U2 had convinced New York that they were real, not press-agent hype. But America is a big country, and they'd have to repeat that performance every night for a long time to make an impression on the thousands of skeptics and millions who'd never heard of them across the continent. They set out to do just that, the hard way. They spent the next three months on an exhausting juggernaut, playing every conceivable stage.

When McGuinness told Premier Talent the boys wanted to start small, he wasn't kidding. The first half of the tour found them in small clubs and bars scattered across the country, places where no one had heard of U2, or cared either. It was a bare-bones tour, with the band piling into a station wagon after an exhausting performance to drive to the town where they'd appear the following night. No venue was too small or inappropriate. They even played bars where they had to compete with wet tee-shirt contests for attention.

Despite the exhausting schedule, they were having a great time. The United States seemed more receptive to them than the people of England. They'd drop in on record stores and radio stations, do a little sightseeing, or just meet and talk to people if they could grab a couple of hours. Yet anyone who looked for the band after the show thinking they could "party" with them was in for a disappointment. They didn't seem to be interested in the usual temptations of tour life.

They also had plenty of time to talk about the future. Bono and Edge, in particular, had a project they'd been getting more excited about now that they had some hope of establishing themselves.

Mindful of the terrible time they'd had getting signed, they often talked about helping other worthy bands— those not considered commercial—get a public hearing.

Their answer would be their own record company, to be called Mother. It would be like Tamla Motown, the soul label that developed a trend-setting formula of signing, developing, recording, and marketing talent. And with U2 getting more popular, Bono and Edge decided that Mother wasn't just a pipe dream. They already had some people they wanted to work with. There was Murphy, a black Irishman with a tremendous voice. Another was John Lydon, former lead singer of the notorious but now-defunct Sex Pistols. They were also interested in "dub" music, the scratchy inner-city rhythm that kept dance clubs in motion; only it would be dub music with a difference—they wanted to use traditional Irish instruments.

Meanwhile, they were getting an education on life in America.

At one date in Texas, McGuinness asked the club owner to pay the band in cash. Cash? . . . The owner pulled out a pistol to add a little emphasis to his answer. The band would be paid by check, just like everybody else. Welcome to the U.S.A.

Yet as they inched their way across the map, U2 found they weren't as anonymous as they'd been even a month before. *Boy* was getting airplay on a host of college stations across the country, and some progressive commercial stations were adding it to their playlist. It had entered the *CMJ* college album charts in mid-March and climbed to number 5 a month later.

Ever mindful of the business side of music, they began to refer to "rack" 'n' roll rather than rock 'n' roll, the racks being the all-important bins where records are displayed in record stores.

Their cause wasn't hurt any when *Rolling Stone* came out with a feature on the band called "U2—Here Comes the 'Next Big Thing,'" filed by James Henke, the journalist who'd enjoyed their company at the Greek restaurant in London.

"U2 is a band to be reckoned with," Henke stated. "Their highly original sound can best be described as pop music with brains. It's accessible and melodic, combining dreamy, atmospheric qualities of a band like Television with a hard rock edge not unlike The Who's. In particular, Edge's guitar playing and Bono's singing stand out; the lyrical guitar lines slice through every song, while the vocals are rugged, urgent, and heartfelt."

U2 had been hard at work for several years, touring and putting out less-than-perfect singles and an EP. But most American audiences were hearing only the music from their brilliant debut and now were anxious to see who had created this overwhelming sound.

At each stop, they found growing numbers of fans who dubbed U2 their favorite band.

But they were still linked to the import bands they'd tried to separate themselves from. Bono insisted to audiences, "We're not just another English band passing through this town of yours." When the sets ended, no one doubted his word.

By the time they hit San Francisco, Bay Area residents were already familiar with U2. Howie Klien, a local music industry figure and DJ, had been on top of the band from the time he heard their first import single. "I Will Follow" had been getting airplay on KUSF, San Francisco's top progressive station, as an import, and *Boy* was added to the playlist after its release. U2 had a Bay Area following sight unseen.

Their first show was at San Jose State College auditorium. "Sold Out" doesn't describe the overcapacity crowd wedged into the auditorium. People were hanging off staircases leading to the balcony, and more were outside still trying to push their way in.

Once exposed to *Boy*, no one could deny the band's unique power and vision. But who could have imagined what they heard on record was only a crude approximation of the band in concert?

California is, among other things, a land of potential earthquakes. Public buildings are erected with these calamities in mind, and so the floor of the auditorium at San Jose State College is set on giant steel springs; in the event of an earthquake, the floor has a slight give to survive the massive forces acting on it.

The night U2 played, the earthquake was inside! Moved by the music, the audience became a single being, stomping, swaying, and shaking. The floor, sitting on its Atlas-like springs, began to move. As the music reached its peak, the floor was moving up and down six inches in time with the crowd and the beat. The San Jose State gig was followed by two sold-out nights at the Old Waldorf, a Victorian-style theater owned by Bill Graham.

The tremendous response was only one reason U2 enjoyed the Frisco stop. Opening the show each night was a local group, Romeo Void, fronted by the larger-than-life Deborah Iyall.

Unlike many headliners, U2 takes a strong interest in their opening bands. Whether it's from memories of shabby treatment early in their career, or their innate sense of grace and manners, the interest is in stark contrast to how support acts are typically treated.

Headliners usually can't be bothered with their support bands. The warm-up act barely gets enough time for a cursory sound check. Headliners know that the worse the opening band, the better they'll sound by comparison. They may never hear the opening act play during an entire tour, staying in the dressing room and avoiding contact with the underbill.

This has never been U2's style. Since they've reached the stature where they can tour with whomever they want, they select bands they believe in and whom they like as people. In earlier days they'd pay close attention to support acts anyway, because they're genuinely interested in music.

Standing in the wings at San Jose State listening to Romeo Void, Bono and Edge definitely felt they were hearing something new, and the music was only one part of it. Deborah Iyall had the audience and the boys from Dublin thoroughly enchanted. A large, commanding presence, Ms. Iyall is the kind of woman who doesn't mind telling an audience whatever is on her mind. Bono was impressed with her gutsy panache.

By the time U2's first visit to San Francisco was over, they'd become close friends with Deborah and the rest of Romeo Void, their manager and entourage. It was a case of mutual admiration. Romeo Void's manager and Bono hit it off especially, talking about everything from the history of architecture to international politics.

At the time, Romeo Void was signed to 415 records (named after the local telephone area code), a San Francisco label run by Howie Klien, the Bay Area's first heavy supporter of U2.

Edge and Bono talked to them about Mother Records and the possibility of a joint recording project. Of course, Romeo Void, their manager Sandy, and Howie Klien were all flattered, and they agreed they'd like to keep the door open for any future association. At the moment it was obvious U2 had their hands full with their own exhausting schedule.

They were constantly on the move, offstage and on. Dates had been left open within the three months to schedule shows where *Boy* was getting airplay or where word of mouth was creating a demand to see them. In some cities, they switched their bookings out of clubs and into larger facilities due to ticket demand.

Back in England, fans were curious about how U2 was faring on their American juggernaut. A writer from *Melody Maker*, Paulo Hewitt, dispatched himself to the States to get the answer. He met up with them in Chicago in late April, with the tour half over.

It'd been a month and a half of nonstop motion, zigzagging across the country. They were booked into Park West, the city's premier dance club. WXRT had been paying a lot of attention to *Boy*, and fifteen hundred people showed up to see his parents.

Hewitt, who'd seen the band when they first had gone to London, reported a story of remarkable progress. A year before, the band hadn't even released their first single in England. After what seemed like an eternity of knocking their heads against the English record-buying public, they were finding a warm welcome in America. Even the usually reticent Larry was moved by the rapid advances they were making.

"We started off playing the small clubs and on the next half of the tour we're playing really big places, places the [Boomtown] Rats are playing!"

Losing Their Thoughts

By this point in the tour, they'd been joined by Steve Lillywhite, who came along to help whip some material into shape for their next album. Lillywhite was all for experimentation in the studio, but U2's loose approach was a bit much even for him. He wanted to make sure they were more prepared this time. They'd had five years to get the songs together for *Boy*, and now they'd have only a matter of months to prepare for an album that would have much higher expectations.

"I always said to them, 'When you're on these long tours in the States, before every gig why don't you just jam or do something and write a song and just ease a new song into the set every three or four gigs. Just try something new.'"

On tour, Lillywhite saw that U2's progress wasn't just musical. "They were growing as people, mentally they were becoming aware. For them everything was new and it was like being born in a lot of ways—getting lots of new ideas together."

Many of the ideas found their way into Bono's notebook.

Following Lillywhite's advice, they worked up new material and had ten or more songs in an embryonic state.

Coming up with musical ideas was no problem, but the lyrics didn't come quite so easily. Bono was rarely satisfied with the words or the melodies he'd first come up with, yet he wrote them all down in his notebook so he could go back and refine his ideas a bit at a time. With his mind ever racing, the idea notebook was getting quite full as they made their way across the continent.

Midway through the tour, U2 rewarded themselves with a working vacation. With Lillywhite in tow, they headed to Nassau's Compass Rose Studios, where luminaries from Talking Heads to Robert Palmer had recorded, for a week of sun, fun and recording. Before they took time out to lie on the beach, they went in to record a song called "Fire," with Lillywhite at the controls.

At the peak of their powers from their nightly workouts, yet relaxed by the island's ambience, the recording went better than expected, and they decided to release "Fire" as a single over the summer.

After a few days on the beach, it was time to complete the final leg of their first major American tour. By now audiences realized that as Bono said, U2 wasn't just another English band coming through town. No longer were they battling against indifferent audiences; now the battle was to live up to grand expectations.

Crowds awaited them wherever they appeared. In

Denver they quickly sold out the Rainbow, a fifteen-hundred–seat venue that most English bands couldn't fill on even their third tour. The tremendous reception in the Mile-High City made it a favorite of the tour and began a relationship that was to play a major role in their future recording career.

By the time U2 hit Portland, Oregon, one of the last stops, Bono's notebook was almost completely filled with song ideas, bits of lyrics, and creative thoughts for the next album.

The Portland show was like all the others: a foot-stomping, energizing, sold-out success. But what happened afterward wasn't. The band was in the dressing room receiving visitors. Bono still remembered the entrance of the two strikingly beautiful blond women who came by to say how much they enjoyed the show. When they finally noticed the two women were gone, they realized so was Bono's travel briefcase, containing not only all his money but his notebook packed with the next album's lyrics and song ideas.

Bono's immediate reaction? "It's the three hundred dollars I want back! Keep the lyrics!" he said. The lyrics would prove much harder to replace.

Stolen lyrics or not, U2 was committed to finishing the tour with a bang. They wouldn't be back for at least six months, and they wanted to leave a big impression on Stateside audiences. So they booked back-to-back continent-straddling concerts, one at the Santa Monica Civic Center in Los Angeles and the other in New York's three-thousand–seat Palladium. Filling both venues was an accomplishment in itself. Once the audience was there, driving them wild was a piece of cake.

In New York, they also put in an appearance on Tom Snyder's late-night talk show. While Bono would later crack up journalists with his impersonations of Snyder, he nonetheless gave the host lots of credit for allowing U2, and other struggling bands like the Clash, on his program.

As they headed home, U2 had much to be happy about. The tour was a smashing success (aside from postconcert catastrophe in Portland), and after three months of their working themselves to the bone, *Boy* made it onto the *Billboard* album charts.

OCTOBER

June 1981. U2 was back in Dublin for a short rest. They'd booked Windmill Lane Studio for August, and there was concern about what they'd do when they got there. Thanks to the Portland blondes, the next album was likely to be more improvisatory than the first.

There wasn't time to worry about it. That same month they headed to England for a number of dates, including London's prestigious Hammersmith Palais.

This time they really did have a right to bill themselves as "just back from a smash tour of the U.S.," and every show was sold out.

In July the single "Fire" b/w "J. Swallow," recorded on their break in Nassau, was released. Island Records knew it might take U2 a little time to break open, but even they were beginning to grow impatient at the English record buyer's stubbornness in ignoring U2's charms. Determined to get the band the recognition they deserved, Island spiced up the release with some clever packaging. They issued a limited edition double-pack single that included a bonus disk, with live performances of "11 O'-Clock Tick Tock," "The Ocean," "Cry," and "The Electric Co." The strategy seemed to work. "Fire" made it into the Top Forty, and U2 had their first record on the English charts.

As the August date for entering the studio approached, there was feverish discussion about how to proceed. With everything going down in his notebook, Bono hadn't committed lyrics and other ideas to memory. With the notes gone, the band suffered collective amnesia.

They spent the last three weeks of July rehearsing, working out the ten songs they wanted to record, but when it was time to go into the studio, they were no closer to having any lyrics. Only one song, "I Fall Down," was complete before they went into Windmill Lane.

They decided to put down the music first and worry about the lyrics later. The instrumental tracks went well. Every cut showed how much the band had grown since the last album, how much more self-assured and powerful they'd become, their force rippling beneath the surface, kept tightly in check to emphasize a more spiritual and dynamic sound.

To introduce a Celtic flavor to the music, they asked Vincent Kilduff, a respected local musician, to add oillean pipes and bodhran, traditional Irish instruments, to some of the songs.

Once the basic tracks were completed, it was up to Bono. Lillywhite made sure there'd be plenty of room for Bono's vocal experimentation. Out of the twenty-four available tracks, he left eight open for Bono to record on so there'd be ample space to take a number of different approaches on any one cut and then make comparisons.

Each day Bono went to the studio, having no idea of what he'd be singing. Whatever came out of his mouth as he ad-libbed along to the instrumental tracks would be recorded. Working alone with Lillywhite, he might record five different takes of one song. Lillywhite would listen to each and splice them together into an approximation of what he thought would be a good melody. Bono'd take the composite tape, work on the words some more, and then record it all over again.

Lillywhite spent as much time pacing back and forth in the control room as he did at the console. Some days they didn't get anything done. Bono would arrive first thing in the morning, and Lillywhite would quietly ask, "Sing?"

"No, it's not right today," Bono would answer.

McGuinness came in one day and asked Lillywhite if he'd ever worked with a band like U2 before. Lillywhite just put his hands to his head and sighed. And at fifty pounds an hour, people were getting concerned.

Even Bono, Mr. Self-Assurance, was showing the strain. The daily trauma of trying to rip himself open and let the creativity pour out was taking a physical and emotional toll. As Lillywhite observed, "Bono does have difficulty sitting down and actually writing words out—he sings whatever comes out. It's a very painful process for him—I'm sure he'd admit this—he puts himself through a lot of hardship to come out with what he feels are his best lyrics."

Despite the anguish, Bono felt as if it were all planned, as if again his and the band's commitment and dedication were being tested.

By now he and Lillywhite were willing to try anything. As he scribbled lyrics on the mike stand, he'd work on the bridge of one song, then switch to taking a crack at the verse of another.

Bono expressed the belief that it was best to record under stress. It provided an invigorating element that helped sweep away all pretense and superficiality, allowing him to get to the heart of what he was trying to communicate. He himself wasn't always sure what that was, and would look for it by examining the train of thought he seemed to be following on random vocal tracks.

"I try to pull out of myself things I wouldn't be able to do with a pen and paper. At the front of your brain is a lot of rubbish: You write about things you think you're concerned about, but that may not be what you're concerned about at all."

But if this were the key to creativity, no one else seemed to be comfortable with it. The Edge's evaluation: "A nightmare."

"I just tried to pull out of myself what was really going on in the songs," Bono later explained. "The things you are most deeply concerned about, lying there in your subconscious, may come out in tears, or temper, or an act of violence." In this case, the question was whether they'd come out at all.

As the days went by and the process continued, Bono resigned himself to the inevitability of the events that brought the band to this precarious position. His strong religious belief became his shield and convinced him that no matter how difficult the recording was, it would turn out for the best. The more he let himself go and sang whatever came to mind, the more he found his religious conviction pouring out of him, into the microphone, and onto tape.

Slowly the snippets of lyrics and melodies were getting pieced together. "Gloria," the album's first song, was influenced by Gregorian chants that McGuinness had given Bono to listen to. Bono found himself singing in Latin on the track and went out to find a Latin dictionary to translate his stream of consciousness. He ran into a friend who studied Latin and brought him back to the studio to translate. It turned out Bono's Latin was almost a direct account of his present predicament, the inability to sing or even stand up, a search for words and meaning.

He changed the words to English, but kept the chorus in Latin:

Gloria in Te Domine, Gloria Exultate:
Glory to God in the highest.

"I Threw a Brick Through a Window" was about the anger of a sixteen-year-old who catches a reflection of himself in the window and in a split second sees himself for what he really is, and realizes he doesn't like what he sees.

Not all the songs were so easily interpreted. Originally, Bono felt that "Tomorrow," with its sinister imagery of a black car waiting by the side of the road and a knock on the door, was about the killings in Northern Ireland. It was only months later that he realized it was really about his mother's death.

"I realized that exactly what I was talking about was the morning of her funeral, not wanting to go out to that waiting black car and be part of it."

Larry, Adam, and Edge would drop by to add their encouragement and give their opinion on the work in progress.

The album originally was going to be called *Scarlet*, after one of the songs. It had a very simple lyric: the word "rejoice" sung over and over again. They decided instead to call it *October* after the haunting tune featuring Edge on piano, an instrument he learned for the composition.

"Scarlet" wasn't the only tune to use the word "rejoice"; there was also a song using the word as its title. It wasn't coincidence.

"I used the word 'rejoice' precisely because I knew people have a mental block against it," Bono explained. "It's a powerful word, it's lovely to say. It's implying more than 'get up and dance, baby.' I think *October* goes into areas that most rock 'n' roll bands ignore."

Indeed it did. It seemed to stray, if not linger, into subjects totally taboo in rock: religion and spirituality.

Listening to the playbacks in the studio, U2 found the religious theme of the album overcame the pressure it was created under, communicating a sense of peace and calm, yet there was hard and solid rock holding up the spiritual foundations.

Over at Island Records, Chris Blackwell was sympathetic about the loss of the lyrics but wasn't gung ho on the idea of an album of rock spirituals. But when he heard the finished product, he and the others at Island felt that U2 had produced a much stronger album than *Boy* (which, surprisingly, Island hadn't been too keen on initially).

But there was a different problem to contend with: timing. The Christmas season was approaching, and that meant many releases by the biggest names in the business, all trying to get a piece of the holiday shopping dollars. The album was as ready as it was ever going to be, but why not wait a few months to release it? Then it wouldn't have such intense competition. Blackwell was worried that a lackluster reception could destroy the momentum U2 had been building over the last year.

Here again the promise of artistic control was put to the test. Who cared what other bands were releasing albums? This record was U2's statement at the moment. In February they'd be a different band; they didn't want people hearing something they'd done six months before.

The decision? Release the album in October, with "Gloria" as the single. A video of the song would be made to break into the video music arena.

For the album cover and the video, they chose Dublin's dockside area known as Lazy Acre, where the Grand Canal meets the River Liffey and the sea. It was a run-down, decaying locale that had been a favorite of Irish poets in years gone by. The band set up on a barge moored in the middle of the Grand Canal and invited friends and family to witness the videotaping. In addition to the ground crew, they hired a helicopter for aerial shots. The video eventually got them their first exposure on MTV.

October's release immediately vindicated the band's decision about timing. It entered the British album charts as soon as it hit the stores, debuting at number 11. Within a month *October* had earned a Silver Disc, and it went on to sell 250,000 copies in England.

Now they had two albums on the charts. Ignited by the interest in the single "Fire," *Boy* had finally worked its way onto the list. "Gloria" also charted.

If people were taken aback by the song's blatantly

spiritual message, there was no way of denying the power of the stinging guitar and ethereal yet tortured vocal performance the song was built around.

In spite of the trauma associated with its creation, or perhaps because of it, U2 was very proud of *October*. It was only after its completion that they could put it in perspective.

"I'm much happier talking about *October* now," said Bono, "because now it's clearer in my head. I listened to it last week for the first time in ages and I couldn't believe I was part of it. It's a huge record, I couldn't cope with it!"

Its completion marked a turning point. Lillywhite made it a policy never to record more than two albums with one band; he felt he'd be in danger of stagnation and complacency. Both he and the band agreed they should look for another producer for their next album. U2 also felt it was time to seek some fresh input, to avoid doing things the same way all the time. That was the only way they'd grow. They'd always thrived on risk and challenge, and working with a new producer would help keep that edge. They didn't know what they were looking for, but they were determined to find out.

To support the English release of the album, U2 headed south for an eighteen-date tour of the U.K. It took them from Norwich University on October first to the Hemel Hempstead Pavilion on the twenty-first.

Meanwhile they kept one eye on the United States, where they planned on returning in November. They'd been trying to break the English market open for over a year, with constant touring and ecstatic audiences and a deifying press making them known far and wide. Yet all they had to show for it was a Silver Disc and a couple of singles on the charts, not including the belated popularity of *Boy*.

The reception in the United States was much warmer. *Boy* had peaked at number 5 on college radio, and gotten to number 13 on the progressive commercial station lists before drifting off the charts in August 1981. The fact that their debut album had managed to remain on the charts for five months was extremely impressive, but as far as U2 was concerned, that was old news.

In November U2 returned to the United States for the first half of their tour in support of *October*. To help the cause, U2 did something they hadn't been compelled to do in some time: they played as an opening act on some dates. Economic necessity demanded it; otherwise, they might not have been able to do the tour.

"We're nearly always close to breaking even on the road, but this time we were going to lose too much," Adam revealed. "Then we found out we were going to do a couple of weeks with the J. Geils Band in stadiums."

Opening some shows in Florida and on the West Coast, U2 was exposed to larger audiences than they could have drawn themselves. But they decided they'd still rather headline a smaller venue than play a place twice as large where the crowd had come to hear someone else. If they could afford to, that is.

Their first gig of the American tour was in New Orleans, aboard the SS *President*, a reconverted riverboat that now serves as a Mississippi River–going rock palace. McGuinness's comment? "This is the first time we've ever played a venue and the venue left!"

As they traced their way across the country, there was something reserved in the reception they were getting. The crowds were as enthusiastic as ever, but from critics and industry insiders, reaction to *October*, and consequently the band, wasn't nearly as positive as it had been for *Boy*.

There's something often called the Sophomore Jinx, or the Second Album Syndrome. It means the band's first album is great, but the second one stinks. Why? Because bands often spend years developing the material for their first album. They write reams of songs as they develop their sound and search for a contract. The songs get refined, honed, and only the best survive to make it onto

Clockwise from top left: Larry marks time, Bono signs, Adam poses, and the band plays on.

ANDREA LAUBACH/RETNA LTD

Below: The Edge has never had to dress or jump around like a guitar hero to play like one. Right: Making believers out of 100,000 people at the US Festival.

*T*op: The Edge works out on his Explorer. Bottom: "Bono, if you're out there in the audience, please come back onstage."

ROSS MARINO

ANASTASIA PANTSIOS/STAR FILE

ROSS MARINO

ANDREA LAUBACH/RETNA LTD.

Left: Bono is probably wondering if he should jump into the audience or not. Top: Bono is probably wondering if he made the right choice. Bottom right: That was fun! Thanks!

Bono proves he's the most powerful vocalist in contemporary music.

ROSS MARINO

The many faces of Adam Clayton. *Right:* The early hippie look. *Inset, right:* On first major U.S. tour (the shirt says it all). *Bottom left:* Protecting Bono's flanks. *Top left:* The mature bass player gives fans U2's bottom line.

ANASTASIA PANTSIOS/STAR FILE

ROSS MARINO

ANDREA LAUBACH/RETNA LTD.

*T*op: Larry
Mullen, Jr. He'll
let you take his
picture, but
don't expect him
to talk to you.
Right: Bono was
right—sleeveless
shirts are
comfortable!

GARY GERSHOFF

Left: U2 has never needed flashy lights and fancy stage gimmicks to bring an audience to their feet. Below: Bono at the US Festival, before he ascended the scaffolding.

ROSS MARINO

*B*ono's vocal performance gets a hand.

ROSS MARINO

ROSS MARINO

*T*op: Bono drafts a fan for the
U2 auxiliary force. Right:
When U2 started, Bono wanted
to play guitar. He still hasn't
gotten it out of his system.

PETER MAZEL/RETNA LTD

LISA HAUN/RETNA LTD

*A*bove: U2 hates to pose for formal photos. A group shot of the most reluctant pop stars in rockdom. Left: Bono snapped leaving the recording studio, after a hard day's work.

Left: The ever affable Bono tries on the latest in his growing collection of hats. Below: The Edge and Adam were friends for years before U2 began.

U2 *soon after the release of Boy.*

JONATHAN POSTAL/RETNA LTD.

the debut. Critics roar approval, and the casual listener is knocked out by the strong initial showing. While a band is out touring to promote their masterpiece, they realize they've got to go back into the studio to do another album, and they don't have a single new song ready. Some said this was the case with *October*.

Many weren't prepared to write off U2 so quickly. The college and progressive commercial stations still believed in the band. And if anything, the lack of mainstream acceptance only solidified their support from those who'd been heralding the band as the Future of Rock 'N' Roll. *October* had shown up on college and progressive playlists at the beginning of December in the low teens and was slowly moving upward. When U2 hit Boston, headlining a sold-out show at the Orpheum, WBCN carried the show live, broadcasting the message that U2 was alive and well as far as alternative radio stations were concerned. A three-night stand at the Ritz proved New Yorkers were still solidly in the U2 camp. But the Ritz shows were important to U2 for another reason. In attendance was a potential next producer.

Making Tracks to the Top

When the decision had been formalized to seek a new producer, Lillywhite suggested a number of candidates. Others offered their own ideas. Near the top of all the lists was the name Sandy Pearlman, a choice that seemed surprising. Pearlman was the man who literally invented heavy metal, coining the term back when he was a writer for *Crawdaddy*, a pioneering rock magazine.

Since that time, he'd stopped writing about it and started creating it, albeit with an artistry and integrity that was at odds with much that heavy metal stood for. He managed and produced Blue Oyster Cult, the original art/metal band, the Dictators, an underground group of New York metal crunchers, Black Sabbath, and other critically snubbed bands who were redeemed by their association with him. But it was his work with another band with impeccable credentials in search of a beefed-up sound that caught people's attention: the Clash.

Pearlman produced the Clash's first U.S.-released album, *Give 'Em Enough Rope*. The performance he drew from a band not known for its musicianship was astounding. It was raw and powerful, committed and believable.

After listening to the Clash album, U2 and McGuinness were convinced Pearlman could be the man to produce them. What clinched the decision was a coincidence dictated by fate. Sandy Pearlman was the friendly manager of Romeo Void they'd hit it off with so well in San Francisco.

McGuinness called Pearlman from Ireland to ask if he'd be interested in working with U2—at least going into the studio and experimenting. Since Pearlman considered them the best band in the world, he wasn't about to say no.

That night at the Ritz, Pearlman brought along Corky Stasiac, who'd engineered the Clash album for him. The band had left a couple of days open to do some recording, and after the show they discussed plans.

The following Monday morning they were at Kingdom Sound, a studio in Syosset, a small town forty-five minutes east of Manhattan. With their tight schedule, the band wanted to get as much done as possible. They had absolutely no preconceptions about what they would do. Pearlman had them play some of the riffs and snatches of music they'd been developing during sound checks and practices, and they began developing ideas on how to work them together. Pearlman wanted to highlight the band's rhythmic power by creating a piece based on simple interlocking drum patterns welded into a sophisticated polyrhythmic beat.

Both Pearlman and Stasiac were immediately struck by two things about the band. Number one was their

professional attitude. After their working with prima don-
nas and egomaniacal musicians, U2 was a striking change.
They came in prepared to work.

The second thing about the band that impressed them:
technical prowess. To create the complex interlocking
rhythms he had in mind, Pearlman wanted Larry to fill
up every available track with a different drum pattern.
After bouncing the tracks down, combining them to make
more room on the tape, he asked Larry to double the
parts, that is, play them over again so the sound would
be much larger and more powerful.

Very few drummers can double even simple drum patterns throughout a whole song. Unless every beat, rim
shot, and paradiddle is played exactly on time, the rhythm
that's supposed to hold the song together suddenly sounds
sloppy and uncontrolled. Yet Larry was able to duplicate
each part exactly in one take almost every time.

The Edge, meanwhile, coaxed a brilliant sound out of
his old Vox amplifier in five minutes, a feat that can take
more seasoned professionals well over an hour of turning
knobs and adjusting volume and tone. Adam, too, plugged
in and was ready to work immediately.

While the three worked their way toward a final ar-
rangement with Pearlman's input, Bono experimented with
melody lines and snatches of lyrics.

By the end of two days of recording, three instrumental
tracks were down and Bono had almost finished the melody and lyrics to the rhythmic centerpiece. The experiment with Pearlman was turning into a success.

The tracks didn't sound like anything they'd ever recorded before, and that was the point of the project. But
the experiment would have to be put on temporary hold.
They had to fly to California for several shows and didn't
know when they'd be able to get back in the studio with
Pearlman.

"It's ludicrous! We don't know how it's going to turn
out; it'll either be brilliant or an absolute failure," Bono
told reporters curious about their strange alliance with

Pearlman. "If I played it for you you'd say, 'What the hell is that?' It's sort of a psychotic rockabilly song, with a drum figure that runs from beginning to end."

They decided to make time to finish the track.

They had a club date scheduled for early December on Long Island that would be broadcast live on WLIR, and a show the night before, but they told Pearlman to book time at the Studio for the afternoon between the shows.

The day was spent overdubbing guitar lines and vocals. The time for the live broadcast was drawing near, but they couldn't tear themselves away. It took McGuinness, who showed up to see what the delay was, to pry them out of the studio. They summoned a couple of cabs, threw their equipment in, and set off for the Malibu Club, site of the broadcast. Their road crew had the rest of their gear set up, and the band made it onstage with only moments to spare.

The recording wasn't completed, but U2 was impressed with the partial results. They looked forward to getting back together with Pearlman to finish the tracks and perhaps record an entire album—even if it meant dragging him to Ireland.

Heavenly Music

But now they had other things to worry about. A controversy was brewing over *October* and its blatantly religious theme. It was fine for bands to sing the praises of sex and drugs and self-degradation, but singing about God? Why, as far as committed rock fans were concerned, a subject like that was, well, sacrilegious. Interviewers began asking pointed questions about the content of songs like "Gloria," "With a Shout," "Tomorrow," and "Rejoice." The band deflected the inquiries.

"It's easy for people who are not Christians, especially writers who do not understand, to take what we say and misinterpret it," Edge later explained about their reticence.

"To much of the world, even the mention of the name Jesus Christ is like someone scratching their nails across a chalkboard," Bono added.

But there were too many questions, and while they refused to preach, denying their faith was even harder. By the time a reporter from *Contemporary Christian Musician* magazine was sent to interview them in Chicago, they were ready to come out of the religious closet.

He found Edge and Larry backstage at Park West after the show, reading the New Testament and drinking orange juice, hardly the kind of postconcert sustenance most hot rock 'n' roll bands imbibe.

"It's time to talk about it," Edge told him. "I really believe Christ is like a sword that divides the world, and it's time we get into line and let people know where we stand. For a long time we haven't talked to interviewers about the fact we're Christians."

"I can't accept a belief that I just came out of gas. . . . That we as a race just exploded into existence—I can't believe that, and I don't think others can, really," Bono interjected, joining the discussion following his usual postperformance debriefing of the fans.

Now that they'd gone public with their faith, they were anxious to clarify what their faith meant to them. "I'm not religious at all, but I do believe in God very strongly," Bono explained later. "People have got to find their own way. I'm not into standing up and saying, 'Hey, you should be into God!' You don't have to preach about it."

This wasn't the only misunderstanding the band had to contend with. Those that weren't labeling them as a religious band seemed ready to tag them as a "rebel" group, that is, supporters of the outlawed Irish Republican Army. People in the crowd would shout pro-IRA slogans between songs and toss money onstage, presumably meant to help pay for guns and other material necessary to perpetrate the violence that was ripping Northern Ireland apart. U2 found this more upsetting than the "religious" label.

Through all this they had to remember their major mission was reaching the public with their music, no easy task, given the complacency of the American airwaves.

"I talked with a radio programming person who's in charge of 75 stations," Bono told one reporter, "and he was being very honest with me and he said, 'Look, these are conservative times. People don't want to change.' He said he's not in the business of teaching people or being as condescending as that. He's in the business of playing what people want, and he says that people don't want new things—they're frightened of new things!... And he said, 'That's sad, isn't it?'"

Even the fact that some people considered them the great white hope of popular music was of little solace.

"We may well be the future of rock 'n' roll," Bono responded, "but so what? When I go back to Dublin, to my girlfriend it's more of a distraction that I'm in a band than any big deal—and my old man still shouts at me for not doing the dishes before I go to bed."

With their bare-bones travel arrangements, it was hard to take predictions of future glory seriously. One journalist who showed up for an interview with Bono in the Midwest was directed to the parking lot of a shabby motel. There he found U2's lead singer passed out in the back of the station wagon that served as their major mode of transportation. After driving all night to get to their next gig, Bono had been too tired to rouse himself out of the station wagon and resettle in his room.

If they stuck to the major cities, they could have played to packed auditoriums every night. But they wanted to play for people who weren't already sold on U2. There were endless rounds of record signings, radio interviews, anything and everything to get themselves known. Of course, any time the anonymity got to them, all they had to do was book a gig in Denver, New York, or San Francisco. The wild response at appearances in the big towns was getting to be a cliché. With the non–ticket holders outside sometimes rivaling the number of ticket holders inside, reviewers would routinely describe the shows as "hopelessly sold-out." Those reporting on the performance related tales of a spectacle bordering on the miraculous.

The constant work was paying off. *October* was moving up the college and progressive charts, and "Gloria" was becoming an anthem, even more popular than "I Will Follow."

As December drew to a close, U2 returned to Ireland. They'd been on the road for three months without a break, and they wanted to spend the holidays at home. They also had to prepare for a Christmas show at the Lyceum and the first performance in their homeland in over a year.

THE LONG AND GRINDING ROAD

U2's local fans had been waiting a long time to welcome home their conquering heroes. Yet suddenly it looked like it was all over. Reports from Dublin stated U2 were breaking up! After all the hard work, just when they were on the verge of busting wide open, they were throwing in the towel. Fans were shocked. The *Hot Press* printed the story, and now the news was being flashed to all quarters. They reported they'd spoken with Bono, in England with the band preparing for the Lyceum Christmas show, and gotten a statement on the phone confirming the split.

In London, *Music and Video Week* magazine picked up the report, commenting that the band members were "victims apparently of the seemingly endemic complaints of pressure, image making, and general ballyhoo" of the music business.

U2's management and Island Records were getting deluged with phone calls, letters, even petitions. U2 couldn't break up! Not now! How could the group that championed not only their own friendship but the need for everyone to work together be allowed to negate all they stood for by this one rash act?

Fans needn't have worried. U2 was in as much danger of falling apart as the Rock of Gibraltar, and anyone who read the original report in the *Hot Press* should have quickly deduced it was a totally fabricated story, meant to draw chuckles, not protest as *Hot Press* later admitted. Unfortunately, it backfired when thousands who heard the secondary reports took the news to heart.

The remarks attributed to Bono should have tipped off anyone to the hoax. The *Hot Press* article said, in part, "Speaking on the phone from London, an emotional Bono divulged the details. He spoke disparagingly of 'the bloody image making machine,' which had contrived to make the band appear as passionate idealists. . . . 'My heroes are Keith Richard and Johnny Thunders,' thundered Bono. 'I'm no different than anybody else—I want to get rich, famous, and laid, and things aren't moving fast enough.' "

In the "news report," Bono also intimated he would be recording a solo album in the not-too-distant future. Planned title: *Boyo*. When the dust settled, the panic it created underscored how important U2 was to so many people.

There was no doubt now U2 was the biggest thing ever to come out of Ireland. Bigger than the Boomtown Rats or Van Morrison. And certainly bigger than Spud, Radiators from Space, and all the other local groups that had once seemed impressive. Now only the largest venues in Ireland could hope to hold their ecstatic audiences.

But first it was time to give Londoners a Christmas present. Two shows at the Lyceum, December 20 and 21. From the opening "Ticket to Ride" riff of "Gloria" through the sing-along rendition of "We Wish You a Merry Christmas" to the specially prepared "Give Peace a Chance" at the show's end, it was unadulterated magic. Even professional writers were by now stumped trying to describe what happened when U2 played. *Record Mirror* wrote, "U2 played the gig of 1981 and words fail me."

The reporter from *Sounds* found the printed word equally inadequate: "What can I say? That U2 were an experience that defies the written word? That the atmosphere was one of sheer jubilation? Or maybe just that if you missed them live, you missed one of the most joyous and inspiring events of the year."

U2 got a Christmas present of their own. Backstage, they were presented with the Silver Disc they'd earned with *October*.

Now it was time to play for the folks back home. The first two dates took place in Cork and Galway. The show in Belfast was cancelled when the floor of the hall was judged too weak to withstand the onslaught of stomping feet U2 were sure to unleash.

The culmination of the Irish tour was their show at Dublin's Royal Dublin Society Hall on January 26, 1982. No rock band had ever been allowed to play the hall or been able to fill it before. Five thousand lucky ticket holders were treated to the spectacle of what U2 had become in their year away from home. From "Gloria" to the close of "11 O'Clock Tick Tock" and the reprise of "Fire" for the encore, it was a delirious homecoming celebration. For "Tomorrow," U2 brought out Vincent Kilduff to play the oillean pipes they'd used on the record.

Melody Maker dispatched a reporter to the scene, and he dutifully tried to record the spectacle. In the end, he threw in the towel, too, admitting that what he witnessed "has to be experienced to be believed."

Concurrently with the minitour, their early supporter Dave Fanning, host of the midnight rock show on RTE, was conducting his poll of the top fifty All Time Classics of rock 'n roll. U2 captured six places, including the number one spot with "11 O'Clock Tick Tock."

But U2 wasn't resting on any laurels. They were still concerned about their next album and its producer. McGuinness had been constantly in touch with Pearlman. The band was committed to recording in Dublin. With all the time they spent away from home, they didn't want to have to be away for the two-and-a-half months it would take to complete the work. And Pearlman was beginning to voice doubts about whether he'd be able to tear himself away from his commitments in America for that long.

With their triumphant return to Ireland complete, they headed back to the United States to finish the October tour. Uppermost was still the question of producer-to-be. By the time they returned to America, it looked as though Pearlman wouldn't be able to put in the time in Dublin. U2 started thinking about using multiple producers on the album, a smorgasbord of production techniques. If Pearlman could do some of the tracks, they had a couple of people in mind who might be able to do the others. One was Jimmy Destri, Blondie's keyboard player.

McGuinness had gotten together with Destri during U2's last jaunt in the United States, and the two had spent a night, as Destri called it, "dropping hints at each other" about working together. Later he told an interviewer from *Trouser Press* about his talk with McGuinness and said, "If he reads this he'll know I'd really like to produce U2." And when U2 rolled into town in February to play the Ritz again, Destri huddled with them before the show.

The band felt good to be back in America. Especially since *October* had moved into the number 2 position on the progressive charts in mid-February. Even in Texas, where a club owner had pulled a gun on them before, things were changing. Now when they played Austin on Valentine's Day, they packed a three-thousand seater. And instead of seeing pistols, they were invited to attend church services by a local congregation the following day in San Antonio, which they gladly accepted.

Parades and Politics

Yet success on the respected progressive charts was getting to be frustrating. They wanted mainstream acceptance. And after four visits to the United States, it was still elusive. What they needed was something to get them noticed by more than just the hipsters who went club-hopping or paid attention to the latest music business trends. They were tired of hearing the criticisms of *October*. That was only a record. They wanted people to focus on them, U2, and let that shape their opinion. They had a plan for getting people to do just that.

Every March New York City hosts a St. Patrick's Day Parade. And U2 planned on being right in the forefront of this activity. They were going to ride a float, playing live. Perhaps not the traditional Irish marching band that parade watchers were used to, but an Irish band nonetheless. It would be fantastic exposure, and the sheer excitement of taking part in the annual event had the band eager with anticipation.

But the specter of sectarian strife raised its head, casting a shadow all the way across the Atlantic.

Bobby Sands, an IRA member who'd recently died in prison from fasting during a hunger strike, was named an honorary grand marshal of the parade. Suddenly the non-partisan parade was being turned into a political event. U2 wouldn't allow themselves to become pawns of the IRA issue. Their message was to rise above the problems of Northern Ireland, not to take a stand on one side or the other.

McGuinness got together with the parade organizers at an Irish bar in New York and tried to convince them to remove Bobby Sands's name from association with the parade. But the organizers were adamant. So was McGuinness—U2 would not appear in the St. Patrick's Day Parade. The senseless hatred they tried to defeat with their music had temporarily gotten the best of them.

It looked like there'd be no shortcuts to recognition for U2.

Instead of playing for all of Manhattan, U2 appeared at a hastily arranged St. Patrick's Day Concert at the Ritz, their favorite N.Y.C. stomping grounds. It was a joyous celebration nonetheless, opening with bagpipes and closing with a rousing version of "Let's Twist Again."

Speaking of celebrations, to keep their name in front of their British fans, they released the single "A Celebration," produced by Steve Lillywhite, in England in March, backed with "Trash Trampoline and Party Girl." It moved up to position number 47, giving the band their third chart single there.

Meanwhile, they were bouncing around America, mostly playing in the same venues they hit on the previous tour. They could have booked larger halls, but U2 always preferred a fully sold-out show in a moderately sized facility to a moderately sold-out show in a bigger one.

When they played the Rainbow in Denver again, the concert promoters took them sightseeing. Lying ten miles outside of Denver is a freak of nature called Red Rocks. Weathered boulders twist and jut from the earth to form a natural amphitheater with perfect acoustics. During the summer, the top names in contemporary music take advantage of the acoustics, and open-air concerts at Red Rocks draws nine thousand people, many coming early to picnic and get a good spot for the general-admission performances.

Accessible only in late spring through early fall, it's not easy to reach. Outside of Denver, already a mile up, the road climbs like an airplane.

As U2 looked around at the massive stones with their strange reddish hue, they were moved by their stark beauty. There was something special here.

"Someday, when you get big enough," the Denver promoters told them, "you can play here."

Then and there U2 vowed they would.

Producing Anxiety

How did U2 survive the monotony and exertion of their ceaseless touring? For one thing, the usual temptations of drink and drugs held no appeal for them, but for another, they genuinely enjoyed traveling, meeting people, and playing their music. Yet by now, on their fifth visit to the States, even U2 was having trouble remembering one town from the next.

Certainly no one was mistaking them for just another punk band anymore. But despite the ecstatic reception to their live shows, they knew they hadn't realized their potential in the United States. Some felt the fault lay with *October*. While it had equaled the sales of the much more highly touted *Boy*, strategically speaking it was only a holding action. U2 was still a band in search of its destiny. The next album would determine the band's fate.

When they returned to Ireland in the spring of 1982, U2 was determined to put the question of their next producer to rest once and for all. They must have read Destri's comments in *Trouser Press*, because he was invited to Dublin to experiment with the band in the studio, much as Pearlman had done. Naturally, they gave him a proper welcome when he arrived, immediately taking him on a pub crawl and introducing him to the band's Dublin. Eventually they settled down to begin work in the studio.

They were in the midst of preproduction, talking about arrangements and ideas, when a call came for Destri from his bandmates back in the States. Blondie had decided to go on the road again (for what was to be their final tour), and they needed Destri Stateside immediately to start rehearsing. Both Destri and U2 were disappointed, but there was little either of them could do.

It wasn't an advantageous situation to be in. They were booked to play a number of European rock festivals over the summer and begin recording in September. They had no time to go hunting for the proper producer for what could very well be their make-or-break album. They called Steve Lillywhite.

"One day they phoned me up and said, 'Look, Steve, you know you said you didn't want to work with us again, and we said yeah that was a good idea—to be honest, we can't find anyone. What are you doing in September?'"

Luckily for U2, Lillywhite was free and agreed to be

behind the boards for their next album.

Bono's report on the conversation is essentially the same. "I rang up Steve, and in a flash he said, 'I'll be right over.' He said we're his favorite group. It's a very close thing."

With a decision made on the producer, the band set off to work their way through the European festival circuit.

At some of these festivals fans from Dublin would arrive in chartered buses, so great was the desire to see their hometown heroes. The strain of trying to reach the thousands of people was audible in Bono's voice.

"The singer is losing his voice," he'd announce on occasion, and then add, "Who needs a voice when it comes straight from the heart?"

The high point of the outdoor dates was the Werchter Festival in Belgium. Sharing the bill were the top names of U.K. rockdom: the Eurythmics, Peter Gabriel, Simple Minds. The event was filmed by Belgium's ID television and film company. Lillywhite came over to mix the band for the sound track, and part of the recording wound up on the flip side of U2's next single, "New Year's Day," several months later.

Unfortunately, part of the recording also wound up on a high-quality bootleg album, *U2: Live*, which instantly became an item every U2 fan had to have. Whether or not U2 made great albums, there was no arguing with the power of their live performances, and the bootleg offered fans what they seemed to want most: an unadulterated documentation of one of U2's many magical shows.

July 31 found the band in Gateshead, England, for an unusual show—U2 wasn't headlining. They were opening for the immensely popular Police at Gateshead International Stadium, but the audience wasn't anxious to get rid of the warm-up act.

By now Bono was sporting the white flag that would join Radar as the band's emblem. "There's only one flag and that's a white flag," he proclaimed. At the end of the show, Bono came back onstage to join Sting in singing "The Invisible Sun," which was appropriate, since Sting's composition was about the Troubles in Belfast.

Clearly, U2 had not been bested by England's biggest band. As *Sounds* magazine reported, "U2 took advantage of the day's upswing to reinforce the numerous claims made on their behalf to be 'the next big thing.'"

For sentimental reasons, however, the biggest show of the summer may have been their performance at a birthday party in Dublin. The Dublin *Hot Press*, the tabloid that stood squarely in U2's corner from the very beginning, was five years old, and the band was happy to play at the party and show they remembered all the help that Nile Stokes, the paper's publisher, had given them; not just in writing about them or in publicizing them, but in believing in them.

In August they took time for a little personal business: the marriage of Bono and Alison, "Allie", as she's affectionately known to those around her. Despite any remarks he'd made in the past about the band being a nuisance as far as she was concerned, Alison has always been very understanding of the fans' desire to be close to the band and sometimes acts as intermediary and retrieves autographs for those desperately seeking contact with U2 after a show.

By the end of August, Bono and Alison were back from their honeymoon, and the band was eager to return to the studio. It seemed like ages since they'd had a chance to record in the orderly, unpressured way that led to *Boy* two years ago.

This time Lillywhite was determined to get the record out of them he knew they could make. They decided to go for a harder, stripped-down "live" sound to showcase the band's awesome power.

Even before they laid down a note in the studio, they knew the album would be called *War*. "It seemed to be the word of the year—every time you opened the papers it was there, and our music tends to draw upon what's happening at the time," Bono said.

They also liked the stark and menacing title because it went directly against the grain of the comfortable image people had of U2. They were idealistic, as *Boy* and *October* had shown, but their idealism was tempered by a sense of reality and urgency about often desperate situations.

The most obvious problem to them was the situation in Ireland, and they addressed it in "Sunday Bloody Sunday." The song was, at least superficially, about the Easter Day uprising in 1916 when British troops killed a number of Catholic protesters. Bono hoped the song would strike a blow for the preeminence of man over movements. But the rest of the band was uncomfortable with the blatant politics of the original lyrics. The strict narration and condemnation of IRA terrorist tactics was eliminated. In their place was a more surrealistic catalog of tragedy and an evocation of the Crucifixion and Resurrection as the Bloody Sunday of the song's title.

Bono later revealed that the song idea first came to him in New York, where he felt compelled to make a statement about the tension he felt in the air around him.

"Seconds," a combination of ska, funk, and laid-back boogie, was inserted afterward to keep the album from getting too dirgelike. But the message is hardly as up as its sound. It's a dreamlike black-humor tale of atomic bombs and destruction. Lillywhite was especially pleased with the drum sound they got on the track.

"New Year's Day" was written in homage to Poland's Solidarity movement, to greet the news that martial law had been lifted in Poland on New Year's Day; obviously nothing had changed. Yet the lyrics speak of faithfulness across time, and Bono's voice carries a tortured hope for reunification.

The hard-Edged guitar sound didn't come easily. Edge had no trouble overdubbing the ethereal, pretty guitar tones he was famous for, but that wasn't what they were looking for on this album. This was *War*, and they wanted it to sound that way. After the gorgeously played takes, Bono would coax Edge onward, urging him to deliver a hot, aggressive sound.

"Whenever we did something on that album it was, 'Hang on, let's make it hard,'" remembered Lillywhite.

Meanwhile, the band was going through a war of their own: Personality problems.

Adam, the single nonreligious member of the band, had always been something of the odd man out as a result. Mild-mannered by typical rock-star standards, his love of a good time nonetheless stood out like a sore thumb against the background of the other three's devout manner. The difference in outlook caused problems before. Only being named best man at Bono's wedding had reassured him of his future with U2, though Bono later admitted U2 came close to breaking up during the recording of *War*.

But in the studio, conflicts were arising again.

Adam did his best to remain a party animal in the midst of U2's rock asceticism. The further Adam got into the typical rock life-style, the further the other band members withdrew from it, as though to balance its impact. This led to a good deal of tension.

Part of the tension was the result of the limits toward which U2 always pushed themselves. They felt they owed themselves and their audience to always go to the edge of possibility. Even, as Bono commented, toward things that frightened them.

To top it off, Lillywhite had a health crisis—toward the end of the project he began losing strength and finally had to be hospitalized before the album was finished. With his health at risk, the staff at the hospital couldn't understand his preoccupation with the unfinished recording.

"What's more important," they asked him. "This record or your health?"

"I'm sorry," he answered. "It's this record."

While he was convalescing, Bill Whelan came in to

oversee the recording, earning production credit for "The Refugee." The band used the lull to bring in the background musicians they'd planned to use.

On "Sunday Bloody Sunday" and "Drowning Man," Steven Wickham added electric violin. Kenny Fradley added trumpet to some tracks, while Kid Creole and the Coconuts' backup singers put vocals on "Surrender" and "Red Light."

Finally released, Lillywhite rejoined the band, and they worked literally up to the last minute finishing the album. "40," their hymn to peace taken from the Fortieth Psalm, was recorded during their final night in the studio, which they had booked until seven A.M.

"It was incredible—Bono singing '40' with this other band waiting outside!" remembered Lillywhite.

They hadn't even started mixing the album yet.

By mid-November it was finished. It had the more stripped-down sound the band had been searching for, and it also contained an astounding collection of powerful, mature songs.

They decided to put Radar on the cover, hoping to offset the strident tone of the album with a picture of innocence and youth.

Their feelings about *War* were so positive that they wondered if they could trust their own judgment. They'd have ample opportunity to get other people's reactions— with a short tour of England, Europe, and Ireland booked in December to debut the new material.

The white flag was now established as their new standard. Bono described its selection as a symbolic gesture. He was sick of the banners people were rallying around. The green, white, and orange of Ireland. The Union Jack. The Stars and Stripes. He wished that the colors would be drained from them all, leaving only a white flag. And he thought a lot of other people felt the same way—people in U2's audience.

Meanwhile, CBS Ireland, which still had a contract with the band that covered only their homeland, issued a limited-edition four-pack retrospective of singles under the name *4 U2 Play*. It contained original *U2 Three* EP songs, along with "Another Day," "11 O'Clock Tick Tock," and "I Will Follow," pressed on color vinyl and offered in the original picture sleeves. It became an instant collector's item.

Tickets to the six dates they'd booked in England sold out immediately, with people waiting in line overnight to buy them. They began in Glasgow on December 1. Then it was on to Manchester, Leicester, Birmingham, and then London, playing both the Lyceum and the Hammersmith Palais on successive nights.

The Alarm was in support, but it was hard to hear how they sounded through the shouts of "U2" that drowned out their performances.

With white flags, smoke machines (used during "New Year's Day"), and powerful new songs, U2 was concerned with the staging as well as the sound of their shows, and they needed someone experienced in the logistics of playing larger venues to handle the equipment and other problems that were growing along with their popularity. They found him in London.

Dennis Sheehan, an Irishman himself, had learned his craft from the bottom up. After starting off playing in bands, he moved behind the scenes, becoming a roadie for a series of bigger and more established groups, culminating in his work with Led Zeppelin. McGuinness heard that Sheehan was probably by this point the top tour director in the British Isles and arranged to meet him in London.

English roadies are famous not only for their efficiency but for their loud, boisterous, and often disheveled manner. So McGuinness was quite surprised to answer the knock on his hotel-room door and find a large man, clean-shaven, sporting a shirt and tie. Could this really be the best roadie in England? Over the next two weeks, the band found out he was and asked him to join up with them on a permanent basis. He's been with them ever since.

   The new songs were greeted enthusiastically, especially "Sunday Bloody Sunday," which Bono often introduced by saying, "You'll probably never hear it on the radio."

   In Europe the response was also great, except that not understanding English too well, the fans were more comfortable with the older and more familiar material. But the real test would be the response in Ireland. So much of the material was inspired by, and written for the people in their homeland, that they would be the ultimate judges of the new songs. As the tour chugged through the last of the European dates, and then through Cork and Galway, the unspoken question on everyone's lips was "What will happen in Belfast?"

   Belfast is the epicenter of the Troubles.

   It was in this violence-torn city that U2 would put their vision to the test. In Belfast everyone takes a stand on one side or the other. U2 wanted to see if they could change that. In a city built on division, was there any room for a message of unification?

   On the way to the hotel, Bono witnessed a tableau that summed up the sad course that had taken possession of the city. A drunk was mouthing off to a soldier, verbally assaulting him in an alcoholic rage. Finally the soldier hit the drunk with his rifle butt, knocking him unconscious. Bono was struck not by the political aspect of the act but by the sadness of it, the horrible chain of events that had led to this and a thousand other brutalities. Later on, he told people he especially felt sorry for the soldier. Yet at the same time he could report to a journalist, with complete sincerity and conviction, that he found real warmth in Belfast.

   They were booked into the Maysfield Leisure Center, a three-thousand seater, and the set was going well, but the real test would come with "Sunday Bloody Sunday." Midway through the set, it was time. Bono was as nervous as he'd been for their first gig in the Gaiety Green car park. He told the audience they were about to play a song he'd written for them, for the city of Belfast. If they didn't like it, he said, U2 would never play the song again. And, he stressed, it wasn't a rebel (pro-IRA) song.

The four of them seemed to draw a collective breath; then Larry snapped into the martial beat, and they plunged into the song. The crowd strained to hear the words. Something about a battle. The chilling weariness of a survivor, a witness. And then the chorus. It was a revelation! The crowd's isolated shouts now grew into one. Fists plunged into the air. Not fists for or against but hands raised together. The band took the audience's energy and sent it back, like images multiplied in facing mirrors, till the song ended in a rapturous explosion of shouts and applause.

After the show, the band admitted to one another that it hadn't been the best of their performances, but the crowd's reaction more than made up for any rough edges. Then, as usual, they played host to some of the fans who came to talk to them.

In Belfast youngsters have to grow up fast, and everything has an aura of urgency about it. Even music isn't something just to be enjoyed, or listened to for a good time. Some of the fans this night told U2 how comforting and uplifting it was to listen to their albums when friends were killed in the Troubles.

They finished with three nights in Dublin, playing the TV Club; it couldn't possibly hold a tenth of their fans, but U2 wanted to show they remembered their roots.

With the reception they got on their short tour, the band was more confident than ever about their new material and about the growing theatricality of their performances. They wouldn't play small clubs anymore, intimate venues where they could practically look every member of the audience in the eye. Bono felt compelled to make ever grander gestures to reach every corner of the large halls they were filling. With his white flag unfurled, he had a prop to amplify his physicality. But even that wasn't enough. He was spending more time offstage than on, climbing about the speakers piled toward the ceiling on either side of the stage, wading into the crowd, singing from their midst. It was Bono's way of maintaining the intimacy with an audience that U2 had thrived on since their earliest days, one that was increasingly threatened by success.

And success certainly seemed to be in the air. In January 1983 they released the first single, *New Year's Day*, from their upcoming album. The album's strongest cut, "Sunday Bloody Sunday," was deemed too emotionally charged to be released as a single in England and was certain to be avoided by the BBC. It didn't matter. "New Year's Day" immediately shot up toward the top of the charts, giving U2 their first Top Ten single in England. On the cover of the single, again a bare-chested Radar.

Advance word from those who'd been privileged to hear rough pressings of the album was creating expectations of mountainous proportions.

In the midst of it all, the band exuded a sense of calm and serenity, like the eye of a hurricane. To support the album, they'd booked another English tour, covering twenty-seven cities in only a few more days, beginning at the end of February. They took to the road and waited for the storm to hit.

THIS MEANS WAR!

War was released on the last day of February 1983, and the dam burst open. It entered the charts at 2, immediately giving U2 their first British Gold Disc. The close-up of Radar on the cover seemed to sum up the state of U2: not little boys anymore but defiantly refusing to give up the innocence and hope that served as their protection in a grown-up world,

Spurred by the success of *War*, *Boy* and *October* reappeared on the album charts.

U2 was already on the road, their official *War* tour having opened in Dundee, Scotland, on the twenty-sixth. In support was an unknown band from America U2 had invited to join them.

Back on their first juggernaut through the United States, the Nitecaps had opened several shows in the Northeast. Led by Jahn Xavier, an energetic white soul singer no older than the lads themselves, U2 had been quite impressed with the group. Now the Nitecaps had just released their first album, and U2 wanted to help get them some exposure. The young American band certainly had its hands full trying to break through to the highly partisan U2 fans.

The public's unbridled enthusiasm for U2 was reflected in Bono's performance. Climbing on sound towers or ven-

turing into the audience was no longer enough. If there
was a balcony in the house, he could be found in it. He
would leap up on the balcony railing, the crew would
throw him the microphone, and he'd sing as he precar-
iously walked along the edge. It was the perfect metaphor
for what the band was all about. Willing to take risks,
exposed and vulnerable, yet completely sure of themselves.

As the band vamped during the middle of "Electric
Co.," Bono teetered along the railing singing "Send in the
Clowns."

Such was the demand to see them that they had to
double back several times in the tour, playing the same
city over again. Reaction in record stores was just as
feverish as in the concert halls. U2 released their second
single from the album, "Two Hearts Beat as One," at the
end of March, and it proceeded directly into the Top
Twenty.

They ended at London's Hammersmith Palais on March
29, 1983. Following the tour, U2 was invited to headline
"The Tube," England's top TV rock show. Big Country
and the Undertones would also be playing. They were
worried their in-studio performance wouldn't translate well
over the little boxes in living rooms all across the British
Isles.

Following U2's four-song set, viewers had no question
that U2 transcended the usual caliber of music on "The
Tube." U2, however, wasn't convinced till they saw tapes
of the program. The director, Gavin Taylor, was able to
capture the essence of the band instead of burying them
in electronic effects. Now even people who wouldn't go
near a rock concert knew there was something special
about U2.

U2 had firmly established itself in England. It was time
to see if they could do the same in the United States.

Waging War in the U.S.A.

When the boys from Ireland last left the United States, a cynic wouldn't be out of place suggesting U2 was no more than a cult band, and one whose eventual success was far from assured.

Listen to what was happening. Depeche Mode. The Human League. A Flock of Seagulls. Gary Numan. People were into machines, technology, synthesizers. U2, with their guitar, bass, drum lineup, was decidedly rear guard. And that second album! Songs about religion? These guys were hopelessly naive! People just weren't buying it.

Look at the numbers. They were getting airplay on perhaps thirty-five commercial radio stations around the country. No matter how loud those thirty-five stations screamed that U2 was the greatest thing since amplifiers, only so many people would hear them. Whether that's why they never sold millions of records or not, there were quite a few people willing to say that as U2 finished up their last American tour, they were on their way out in more ways than one.

All that talk ended on New Year's Day.

Among their fervent followers, excitement had been building in the band's absence. As soon as "New Year's Day" was released in England, it got radio and dance-floor play as an import. The dance-floor DJs who'd been fed up with the dispassionate synthesizer doodlings heard a record people wanted to dance to. And radio stations heard a record people wanted to listen to.

At WLIR in New York, "New Year's Day" was voted Screamer of the Week by listeners the first week of the year, a typical response. It showed up on the college album charts—the one song was getting more play than many hit albums, with eight or nine different cuts to choose from. U2 had spent two years playing every conceivable stage, except, of course, the large ones. After all that long, hard work, they were about to be accused of being overnight sensations.

War was released in the United States in March, debuting on the commercial progressive chart at number 10, and by April U2 was back in the States for another three-month tour.

They were, as one says in the industry, "happening." No longer the almost-tentative band they'd been when they first crossed the country, they'd grown as musicians, as people, as performers. Edge and Adam may have still remained rooted in place, but their presence had grown to match their enlarged surroundings.

The first time through the States, they used to huddle together on the bigger stages, seeking comfort in one another's company. Now they were completely at ease, smiling, laughing, reveling in the sheer exuberance of what they were doing, and giving people a chance to share the joy, not just observe it.

Bono was the one who'd really grown into his part. He danced across the stage, climbed up any mountable structure in the hall, dragged fans onstage to dance and sing. And the white flag flew over it all.

People came waving signs, bearing flowers, and flying white flags of their own. It was a genuine rock 'n' roll revival meeting.

The release of *War* the month before had immediate and dramatic impact. All the rock stations sat up and listened, not just the progressives. "New Year's Day" was getting airplay across the country. And MTV put the video of the song into rotation.

Island Records and U2 spared little expense in creating the haunting and evocative video filmed that winter. U2 portrayed themselves as musical partisans, liberationists on horseback, singing their song amid a white-blanketed wasteland. Interspersed World War II battle footage added an air of uneasiness and uncertainty, giving the clip a stark, menacing beauty.

U2 was finally getting a fair hearing. By the end of April, *War* had moved into the Top Twenty on the *Billboard* album charts and was #1 on progressive stations. They earned their first American Gold Record (sales of five hundred thousand copies). When they hit New York, they were booked into three sold-out nights at the Palladium.

Shortly before *War*'s release, Island Records had changed distributors; Atlantic Records replaced Warner Bros. Yet Warner execs still came to the New York dates, showing that even those in the jaded record business knew U2 was more than just "product." The band remarked on how good that made them feel.

They were reveling in their growing stature. Responding to the crowd's tumultuous reception, Bono announced, "I used to be afraid of this city, but I never will be again." Later, he borrowed a camera from the audience and started snapping pictures of the crowd, as though he wouldn't believe the enthusiasm unless he had tangible proof. By the time they reprised "I Will Follow" for an encore, the crowd was delirious. They had to stop the song to prevent a riot from breaking out, so high was the level of excitement in the hall. After restoring order, they plunged right back in midbeat, as though it had never been interrupted. This was nothing new—it was getting predictable that fans would be so carried away that the band would have to stop playing momentarily, and they'd gotten quite adept at plunging back into a song where they'd left off, barely looking at one another to pick up the cue.

By May promoters were rebooking the band into larger facilities. The ones originally planned weren't big enough. A far cry from the early days two years ago—when they sought out the smallest clubs in towns where they were unknown.

Some asked if they weren't selling out by playing the ten-thousand–seat halls instead of the more intimate venues in which they'd built their reputations. Bono's response: "If we stay in small clubs, we'll develop small minds, and then we'll start making small music."

To show themselves to as many people as possible, touring large halls was a good way to display the flag. But there were other ways, too.

Rock Music

Ever since the band had been shown Red Rocks, the outdoor amphitheater near Denver, it had been on their minds. They'd said among themselves if they ever recorded a live video, they'd do it there. Now they decided it was time. Not only would it let people see and hear the band as they were in concert, proving they were one of the greatest live acts in the world, it would also reduce the problem of bootleg recordings.

Fans, already addicted to U2 concerts, were buying the growing number of bootleg tapes making the rounds in the underground rock 'n' roll bazaar. The royalties the band were losing was only one aspect of the problem. More important was the lack of quality control. A definitive live authorized record and video would, they hoped, put an end to the bootlegs and give millions of people who didn't attend concerts a chance to see U2.

A live video and album is an expensive proposition. U2 had about fifty thousand dollars in the kitty, and they were willing to spend it all to get the best possible results. They contacted their Denver promoters, Feyline Presents, and told them what they had in mind. They weren't encouraged when the people at Feyline, thoroughly acquainted with live video and sound recording, estimated it would cost a quarter of a million dollars to do it right. The price tag was way over U2's head, even with *War* riding the charts. But the boys weren't easily deterred. It was as though, once again, they delivered themselves up to a greater power and pushed ahead.

Feyline had worked with U2 since their first show in Denver. The company books hundreds of bands every year, from the up-and-coming to the biggest superstars. They knew U2 was different. There was something very special about the band, not just their music but as people. They agreed to help get the video made however they could.

Island Records was brought into the project. Chris Blackwell had to think long and hard about it. He loved U2, but the recording would cost a lot of money, with no guarantee of any kind of payback. What if the band had an off night? What if there were some foulup with the video equipment? A one-shot project like this was a tremendous gamble. But Blackwell believed in U2 too much to say no.

U2, Island Records, and Feyline Presents formed a joint production company called U2 at Red Rocks Associates. Each put up a third of the cost and shared the risk and potential profit. On paper it looked like there was a lot more risk than profit involved. Only an absolute belief in U2 could overcome the logic that said the project should never be attempted.

Under the best circumstances, recording at Red Rocks is a logistical nightmare. At eight thousand feet, it has to be the most naturally high staging area in the country. The grade is so steep the semitrailers that carry the huge stacks of equipment from gig to gig can't negotiate the last several hundred yards of road. Everything has to be unloaded from one truck, transferred to another, and unloaded again. A twenty-four–track mobile studio is used for live recordings. All the recording machines, sound board, and inboard and outboard equipment are built into a big truck: the kind that can't make it up to Red Rocks. A twenty-four–track board had to be found that could be boxed, shipped, and set up on top. Once they finally got everything there, they'd have to build a recording studio to put it in.

It gets worse. The red rocks (they're really sandstone) that give the place its name have an unusual characteristic: they emit a low-level radiation, "radio waves." The thick electrical cables that connect the recording equipment to the stage make wonderful antennae for these radio waves. The cables were going to have to be laid perfectly to keep interference on the recording from happening.

Even the stage would have to be rebuilt. A three-foot fence separated the stage from the audience at Red Rocks, and barriers were something U2 never allowed to stand between them and their fans. A new stage would have to be constructed on top of the regular one, making it the same height as the fence and allowing an overthrust to be built so Bono could walk right into the audience. And try running around the stage like Bono does at eight thousand feet. Oxygen is required at all shows so performers can suck in a few lungfuls to keep from passing out. Most performers slow down to compensate. Bono wouldn't hear of it.

Where were they going to find the time to do all this? They had a heavy tour schedule. They couldn't take more than a day or two beforehand to get all the equipment set up and check everything. Under the best of circumstances, maybe it could be done. But fate had a different set of circumstances in mind.

With so many potential problems, U2 decided to hedge their bets. When they hit Boston in early May, a mobile studio was on hand to record their performance, with Jimmy Iovine (producer of Patti Smith, Stevie Nicks, and Tom Petty) at the controls and Shelly Yakus engineering. They also arranged to record their upcoming performance on Germany's Rockpalast 83, set for late August. No matter what happened on the top of the mountain, there was no sense wasting the opportunity to capture the blistering performance U2 was turning out nightly in more conventional settings.

Meanwhile, preparations for Red Rocks continued. Steve Lillywhite was brought aboard as producer (their mutual agreement about not working together again being confined to studio projects), and Gavin Taylor, the director of the English TV program "The Tube," whose work they had admired, was signed to oversee the video recording.

Early in May, Lillywhite, Gavin, and the Denver promoters gathered for initial site surveys and preproduction meetings. They spent grueling hours going over the details of how they'd record the event and how to overcome the obstacles.

One thing they had little worry about was the size and enthusiasm of the crowd. Denver had always been good to U2. Since their first show at the Rainbow a little more than two years before, the Denver fans had been among the most vocal and enthusiastic. Now with *War* high on the charts, the nine thousand tickets were quickly sold.

U2 got some practice for the large crowd a week before Red Rocks when they played in front of more people than ever before—well over one hundred thousand. It was the US Festival, put together by Steven Wozniak, who'd made millions on the Apple Computer. The three-day festival featured the top names in rock: David Bowie. Van Halen. Joe Walsh. Early on Wozniak decided U2 were among this elite group.

But there was an undercurrent of tension throughout the event. The site of the festival was hot, dusty, and poorly prepared. A financial disagreement broke out between the Clash and Wozniak. Now, on day two, it looked as if the Clash might refuse to play.

The assembled journalists, too, began to feel they were being shabbily treated, and tempers flared throughout the staging area.

The Clash finally agreed to perform. But when they took to the stage, they announced that they were, in effect, playing under duress; they would have walked if it hadn't been for the fans who were there to see them. Joe

Strummer in particular let the audience know he'd rather not be there. It made Bono uncomfortable.

Ever since *War*, U2 was being tagged as a political band. Why was a label always necessary? Why couldn't the music be enjoyed for what it was? Journalists had thrown U2 into more camps than a refugee. Now people were linking them to the Clash. And they were going to think that U2 didn't want to be here either; that somehow, attendance at this gathering was politically incorrect. It was an impression U2 was anxious to counter.

When U2 hit the stage on day three, Bono grabbed the mike and screamed, "Nobody twisted my arm—I WANTED to be here!" They erupted into sixty minutes of one of the most powerhouse performances they'd turned in all tour. Galvanized by the thought of the thousands of spectators—many who knew nothing more about U2 than their name—they roused the crowd into one of the most enthusiastic receptions of the festival.

Bono had examined the jungle-gym–like sound towers flanking the stage, and now he put them to use, carrying his flag up to the top of the tweeters six stories above the stage.

As one journalist giving the play-by-play reported, "U2's sheer enthusiasm and dedication wins respect from the seen-it-all crew as well as the audience. Missing Persons [the band that had to follow their powerhouse set] do not have an enviable job."

They were ready for Red Rocks. But was Red Rocks ready for them?

Three days before the show, scheduled for June 5, 1983, the assault on Red Rocks began. The dawn had broken cold, gray, and rainy, a drastic change from the pleasant spring Denver had been enjoying. By the time the crew got up near eight thousand feet and the unloading, reloading, and unloading of equipment was under way, the weather had deteriorated. The rain increased, and the thermometer headed for the freezing point.

Over the next two days, there was little improvement.

The rain dissipated, replaced by a bone-chilling fog that soaked through every member of the crew. Worse, the puddles of water and dampness created the constant danger of electrocution from the ribbons of power lines snaking through the area. Lillywhite worked feverishly to get the board set up without having moisture send a short through the delicate circuitry. Gavin Taylor brought two cameramen with him from England to supplement Feyline's crew, and they had their hands full eliminating the static in the cables hooking up the five ground-based cameras.

On the afternoon of June 4, the day before the concert, U2 arrived at Red Rocks from an exhausting show in Salt Lake City. The weather was beyond miserable; for this time of year it was a freak of nature. No one had expected anything like the conditions they were encountering, and they were behind schedule. Over the three days of preparation, the mountain was lashed by rain, sleet, and snow. A tornado struck forty miles to the north.

As one of the technical organizers, Doug Stewart, said, "The only thing that kept this whole project on track was the common bond between the band and the production people. Everybody felt there was a principle to this thing, and that was to get down on tape once and for all the truly amazing live performance that U2 was capable of delivering."

All four of the band stayed at the site, though they wouldn't be able to begin a rehearsal for hours. They walked about, checking on preparations, shouting encouragement. Bono seemed to revel in the forces of nature they battled. "This was never meant to be U2 at the beach!" he'd say. The band's entire career had been based on dealing with adversity, and this was one more test, one more obstacle that was meant to be overcome.

At about ten P.M. the night of June 4, they got onstage to check sound levels and finish troubleshooting the newly wired system. They worked through the night, soaked to the skin.

By morning, the weather was worse, and the forecasts didn't look good. It was time to make some hard decisions. It was one thing for U2 to go onstage in a storm in a display of bravura (or foolishness), but what about the fans? There was a chance of physical danger: hypothermia, even frostbite if the temperature kept dropping. Roads would be dangerous. Should the show be cancelled? The equipment packed up and shipped back down the mountain? They called a meeting and devised a plan of action.

That afternoon rock radio stations in the Denver area announced that U2 would play. They'd also perform a free show the following night at the Colorado University Events Center. Anyone who missed the Red Rocks show because of the weather was welcome to come.

U2 fans were no more easily discouraged than the band. Early in the afternoon a steady stream of people began making its way from Denver, dragging chairs and picnic baskets as though it were sunny and warm.

By evening the amphitheater was almost full, and the chilling rain eased a bit. Out of nine thousand ticket holders, fewer than a thousand stayed home. As the sun set behind the massive rocks, U2 took the stage.

How did U2 know that this documented performance was meant to be? Everything was too exceptional for coincidence. The weather—as extreme and unseasonable as had been witnessed in the century. The crowd—a collection of people who knew that not to make the trek up the mountain would be to miss a special moment in rock history. And U2—reaching into their reserves of power and commitment to put on one of the most magical shows of their career.

It's all on the video of U2 at Red Rocks. The smoke rising off the stage isn't from a machine—it's steam and fog rising off the sweating bodies of the band and stage crew. The monoliths on either side of the stage, deluged with lights, reflect an eerie, otherworldly glow.

Atop the rocks, propane torches sent plumes of flames

skyward. On the ground five cameras recorded the action, while a helicopter captured the scene from the air.

Onstage, U2 created one of the most affecting performances of their career. The crowd pressed forward at the first note. Bono sat on the monitors by the apron, singing, grabbing the scores of hands stretched up to touch him. He went out into the audience, danced with the fans, and brought up a bewildered and delighted girl to sing with him. The joy between the band and the audience was palpable. Bono announced, "If you look up at the sky, you may see rain, but all I feel here onstage is sunshine."

The euphoria spread into the recording hut and the director's booth. After three miserable days, the crises and complications, they could see and hear something remarkable happening, and they knew they were capturing every moment.

Early in the planning, the emphasis was put on the performance. This was a show for people, not for cameras. To disrupt the flow of energy between the band and the crowd would be to miss the entire point of a U2 show. There would be no second takes, no blocking of sight lines to get a better camera angle. And it was all paying off.

By the time the band left the stage after leading the crowd in a final singing of "40," the rain had stopped.

"I go to hundreds of concerts a year," Doug Stewart, the production coordinator, said, "and I KNOW, no matter how many concerts I go to the rest of my life, there will never be another one where the interchange of energy between the audience and performers will ever be any stronger than it was at that show. It was just absolute magic."

The band, the stage crew, and the production people— were walking around dazed after the show, unable to comprehend or deny the power of what they'd witnessed and created. When they descended the mountain, unwilling to let go of the moment, they all repaired to a restaurant and discussed everything that happened a thousand times over, convincing themselves it really occurred. By the time they went outside, the sky had cleared. Every star was in sight.

The next night, true to their word, U2 played a free concert at Colorado University.

Another successful tour. *War* had broken them wide open. They were filling larger halls, playing to audiences who came not to see a rock show but to see U2. It was time to go home.

KINGS OF THE CASTLE

*U*2's homecoming wasn't going to be a private affair. They were slated to headline an outdoor festival called A Day at the Races, at Dublin's Phoenix Park racetrack in August. Thirty thousand people were expected for the all-day event.

U2 was more than just Ireland's top band; they were a source of national pride, a mouthpiece for the country's problems: the religious strife, the unemployment, the growing menace of drug abuse.

Recognition even came from Ireland's prime minister, Dr. Garret FitzGerald, who'd recently asked Bono to serve on the Select Government Action Committee on Unemployment.

Bono first met the prime minister at the London airport where both were waiting for a flight to Dublin. Bono engaged the PM in a discussion-cum-argument about the nation's problems and policies, and the two had kept up a correspondence since.

When Bono's presence on the government committee was requested, it was quickly accepted, but he later found the experience disillusioning and asked to be relieved of his responsibilities.

"There was another language I had to come up with, which is 'committeespeak.' I could go off and right wrongs and go into a committee, but that's not where I am. . . . I think you've got to find your place. It may be on a factory floor, or it may be in writing songs—when you're where you should be and you know it in your heart—that is when you're involved."

In the days before the show, excitement built to a fever pitch. Reservations for seats on the tour buses bringing people from all over the British Isles quickly sold out. Radio, TV, and newspapers carried running accounts of the upcoming event as though it were the most important story of the year, not an afternoon of music. On the radio Jim Kerr, lead singer of Simple Minds, who were scheduled to play, expressed relief that he wouldn't have to follow Bono's performance.

Yet the show was fated to be marred by events emanating from the Troubles. A week before, Thomas Reilly, Bananarama's road manager and a popular figure on the Dublin music scene, had been shot by a soldier in Belfast. Several disturbances followed the shooting, and the violence was on everyone's mind as they filed into Phoenix Park on Sunday, August 14, 1983.

Opening the show was a duo of traditional Irish singers, followed by Perfect Crime from Northern Ireland. Steel Pulse was next and then the Scottish band Big Country, now tagged as a U2 clone, took the stage and proved they had an identity of their own.

It was ironic that Stuart Adamson, their guitar player, was accused of ripping off the Edge's style; when U2 first started getting attention, Edge was accused of copying Adamson's style, which he'd developed in the Scottish band the Skids.

It was a beautiful day, but many weren't willing to let the clear sky erase their partisan feelings. The Eurythmics played next, and during their set a group near the front heaved firecrackers onstage chanting, "English bastards!" Lead singer Annie Lennox did her best to cool out the crowd.

Finally after a well-crafted set by Simple Minds, the

crowd got what it was waiting for. The MC swaggered to the mike and asked, "Do you want to hear the best in live music?" Shouts of joy and anticipation split the air. "Last December was the last time Bono, the Edge, Adam and Larry played in Ireland. In six short months U2 have conquered the world!"

The crowd roared as the four took the stage. From the moment they launched into "Out of Control," the audience was in the palm of their hands. Bono didn't need a microphone, the way the crowd sang along to every song. A large white flag was waving in the audience, and Bono asked for it to be passed up to the stage. Amid chants of "Ireland, Ireland!" he carried it to the top of the sound towers on "Sunday Bloody Sunday." Leaving the white flag symbolically flying over the assembly, he dedicated the next song, "I Fall Down," to Jim Reilly, Thomas's brother and himself a popular figure as the drummer of Northern Ireland's Stiff Little Fingers.

Midway through the set, Bono announced that it was Edge's birthday (it had actually been the previous week), and the crowd joined in singing "Happy Birthday" to the reluctant guitar hero.

Finally, for the last encore, Bono brought out Annie Lennox to join him and the audience in singing the antiwar anthem "40." The crowd remained long after U2 left the stage. Backstage, Jim Reilly rushed to embrace Bono, saying, "Bono, you've given me strength."

The summer and fall were spent playing scattered dates around Europe, like the Rock Pop Concert Festival in Dortmund, Germany, that was filmed and shown on TV through most of Western Europe. The rest of the time was devoted to readying the release of their live album and video, now titled *Under a Blood Red Sky*, from the supernatural glow that suffused the night in June. They had to make some hard choices. The video looked and sounded great, but some of the songs had been captured even better at the live recordings in Boston and Germany.

They decided to go with the best-sounding recordings no matter where they came from. When the album was released, November 21, only two songs, "Gloria" and "Trash Trampoline and Party Girl," were from the Red Rocks show. "11 O'Clock Tick Tock" came from Boston, while all of side two, "Sunday Bloody Sunday," "The Electric Co.," "New Year's Day," and "40" were from the Rockpalast. Jimmy Iovine was credited as the album's producer.

Under a Blood Red Sky entered the British charts at number 9, and by the second week was in the number 1 position. To give it a boost, U2 took a hefty cut in their royalties making it possible to lower the price of the album and passing the savings on to record buyers.

The band wasn't around to bask in the glory. They were half a world away on their first visit to Asia. On November 13, U2 left Dublin en route to Japan, with a stop in Honolulu for a performance and a few days' relaxation. They were looking forward to the visit to Japan, especially because of an encounter they'd had during their last stop in Chicago.

Exhibiting Pacifism

Chicago is the home of the Peace Museum, an organization dedicated to promoting international understanding and nonviolence. The museum planned an exhibit called "Give Peace a Chance," documenting the role of popular music in the peace movement. People like Yoko Ono, Bob Dylan, Joan Baez, Pete Seeger, and many others had pledged their support. And what better currently popular band to represent these ideals than U2?

The exhibit curator contacted Terri Hemmert, the WXRT disc jockey, an early U2 supporter, and she arranged a meeting with the band when they played Chicago. It took place in their hotel coffee shop. U2 was instantly enthusiastic about the exhibit. They were also interested in the museum's other work and asked to be taken on a tour.

The current show was called The Unforgettable Fire. Considered a national treasure in Japan, these were paintings and drawings done by the survivors of the nuclear attacks on Hiroshima and Nagasaki. The horrific visions the drawings recorded made a tremendous impression on the band. Another exhibit was dedicated to Martin Luther King and his nonviolent struggle for black equality.

U2 pledged to do all they could to help and, as the tour progressed, kept in touch with the museum, making suggestions and offering items for the upcoming exhibit. They donated the original manuscripts of "Sunday Bloody Sunday" and "New Year's Day" and white flags Bono carried onstage during their performances.

They also wanted to build a scaled-down mock-up of their concert stage. The idea was to show that everyone could do something to work for peace. For U2, that meant getting up onstage and singing about it.

As the band headed to Japan, the land of the Unforgettable Fire, they shipped off another item for the exhibit: the original stage backdrop with Radar's picture that had been the band's symbol from their first major tours.

Their first show in Japan was in Osaka on the twenty-second, then on to Nagoya before finishing with a four-night stand in Tokyo.

U2 was used to the adoring fans that go hand in hand with popularity, but they weren't prepared for the unrelenting attention they got in Japan. It seemed as if they were performing before an audience every waking moment. Their movements from city to city were publicized as news events, and crowds followed them everywhere and were lying in wait to catch a glimpse of them at railway stations and hotels. They wondered to themselves how the Beatles managed to cope with the unending scrutiny.

Concerts, too, were a bit problematic. In Japan audiences are required to stay in their seats, and there's always a bevy of security guards to enforce the rule. But it's easier to stay in your seat for some groups than for others. At Osaka, despite the rules and the security, the crowd couldn't be restrained and started rushing the stage. The manager of the hall rushed the stage, too, screaming that the show had to be stopped.

Dennis Sheehan tried to reassure him everything was all right: this was just the standard response to U2. It was only later they realized they may have cost the hall manager his job.

By December 18 they were back in London at the Apollo Victoria Theater for the Big One, a benefit concert for the Campaign for Nuclear Disarmament. It was a star-studded evening—Ian Dury, the Alarm, Style Council, Elvis Costello, and more. But U2 was headlining.

It wasn't just The Bomb Bono was concerned with this evening; the day before, Harrod's department store had been bombed by the IRA, killing several people. Bono reminded the audience that nuclear war wasn't the only problem of violence they should be concerned with.

At the end of their set, Mike Peters from the Alarm joined U2 onstage, singing "Knocking on Heaven's Door" and "40" with them.

They returned to Ireland to spend a quiet holiday season at home and take a well-deserved break.

In January 1984, *Under a Blood Red Sky* went platinum in England, one of the few live records ever to do that. *War* was still riding the charts a year after its release. But they were thinking about their next album. They'd been thinking about it since before the debut of *War*.

They didn't want to be caught producerless at the last minute again. It had always been something—no lyrics or no producer or not enough time in the studio. This time they vowed to avoid all these problems.

The Board Game

They wanted a producer who would become totally involved in the project. Not only with the recording but the inception of the material, too. U2 has always represented "we," instead of "us" and "them." That's why they brought people onstage, why Bono used to plunge into the audience, why they stayed to talk to fans after gigs. Now they wanted to break down the barriers separating producer from band.

They planned on an album with an ambient quality forming a complete soundscape instead of a collection of songs. They wanted to find someone who'd feel free to play an instrument on some tracks or help shape ideas as they were first taking form. Who was most qualified to turn this musical vision into reality?

A number of names popped up. Jimmy Iovine, who'd produced some of the recordings on *Under a Blood Red Sky*, was one. So was Glyn Johns, producer of the Rolling Stones, the Who, and the Eagles. German technopop producer Conny Plank was also mentioned.

Each was contacted, and while things looked promising after preliminary discussions, scheduling problems and artistic differences eventually ruled them out. U2 discussed producing the album themselves but felt that might be premature.

They were committed to trying something different, even if they'd fall flat on their faces. That was the only way for them to keep growing.

One name came up all the time as their version of "In Search of..." continued: Brian Eno. As Edge said, there are four distinctly separate tastes in music and producers in U2, but Eno's name was one that always seemed to meet unanimous approval.

At first blush, it was a strange choice. Eno, Mr. Am-

bient himself, created aqueous textures that some suggested could extinguish U2's fire. Eno had put out "Music
for Airports," a homage to the ultimate in rock Muzak,
a tone poem glorifying the unassuming music that had
kept U2 off the radio for so long.

But Eno was also a man who'd turned his musical
limitations into an asset, as U2 had done early in their
career. Since leaving Roxy Music, he'd collaborated with
leading lights in contemporary music. Talking Heads in
particular had benefited from his shaping and inventive-
ness, and U2 had always been fans of theirs. And of
course, Eno had overseen Lillywhite's first album with
Ultravox.

They rang up Lillywhite to get his reaction to the idea.
He thought it was a good choice. They then contacted
Eno while they were in the United States for the *War* tour.
He immediately told them he wasn't interested. But once
they decided he was the best man for the job, they refused
to take no for an answer. While they talked with other
potential producers, they kept "nagging" Eno, as he put
it, to be the producer. To make sure he was making the
right move in turning them down, Eno listened to some
of their earlier albums and found he wasn't particularly
inspired. The answer was still no.

What to do? Bono decided to put his vocal talents to
use.

They called Eno in a Canadian studio after tracking
him to where he was working on a typically eclectic project: a solo LP by avant-garde pianist Harold Budd. Eno
was busy at the moment but said he'd get right back to
them. Bono and Edge sat by the phone in Dublin waiting
for the call. They weren't about to take no for an answer
any longer.

With Edge shouting his own comments toward the re-
ceiver, Bono spent two hours on the phone with Eno,
explaining what U2 wanted to do and why he should help
them do it.

By the end of the first hour, Eno was pretty impressed.

They certainly had a vision and obviously a great deal of commitment. And while Eno was bombarded with tapes of bands requesting his production services, most of them were synthesized techno bands, interested in him because of his work with Roxy Music and his pioneering pop polyrhythms. U2 was going against the grain. As he hung up, he still wasn't sold on the idea. He told Danny Lanois, his engineer, to get ready to go to Dublin with him to check out a potential production project.

What drew Eno to Ireland? One of the things was curiosity. "I was mystified by their reasons for wanting me particularly, I wanted to discover just what they wanted from me." Eno wasn't the only one who was initially against his involvement with U2. So were Chris Blackwell and others at Island Records.

"We were the goose that laid the golden egg," as Edge observed, "and suddenly we were changing our diet.... They were a little freaked. But even if the album had been a terrible flop, it would ultimately have been the right decision for our growth."

Once he met the band, Eno decided almost instantly to work with them. He later told journalists it was Bono, something about him that made the idea of spending time in the studio with him very interesting. He was intelligent, inspiring. He talked about the band and the recording not so much in terms of instrumental input but of identities, contribution, what each of them added to the whole band. They wanted Eno's help in putting it down on tape.

The search for a new producer had ended.

"Over the last five years every band in the country has been on the phone to Eno, but we were the only offer he accepted," Adam remarked. "And the question shouldn't be why we wanted to work with him, but why he wanted to work with us, this pathetic little rock 'n' roll band from Dublin who hadn't made a good record since *Boy.* He must have seen something there."

Once the choice of Eno had been publicized, there were thousands ready to tell them why it was a mistake.

Yes, to answer skeptics, it would be different, but that's what U2 wanted. As Edge explained, "We needed to take a side step from what was quickly becoming a caricature of ourselves."

"The *War* album was such a success and I love it," admitted Edge, "but it was a bit one dimensional look at the band. We could probably have safeguarded our success, sitting on a fence, but I felt we needed to take a radical step."

A Man's Studio Is His...

It would be a total departure for U2. They wouldn't even use a studio. Instead, they'd record in a place filled with as much atmosphere and mystery as their music.

Lying twenty-five miles north of Dublin, Slane Castle is no stranger to rock 'n' roll. An open-air theater on the grounds has been the site of numerous concerts. Bruce Springsteen and the Rolling Stones have played there. But to the best of anyone's knowledge, the inside of Slane Castle had never played host to a rock band. But U2 was more than a rock band, especially in Ireland. They prevailed upon Lord Henry Mountcharles, an Irish aristocrat who doubled as a U2 fan, to arrange for the band to have access to the castle for six months.

They would take a free-form approach to capturing the spirit of U2, instead of worrying about every bar of music. There would be some sacrifice of technical quality by using a jerry-built studio, but the inspiration and atmosphere they'd draw from the place would more than make up for it.

There were other reasons for selecting Slane. When they tried recording at Windmill Lane these days, it was like a circus; too many friends and fans dropping by. They hoped the twenty-five-mile distance would give them a little privacy.

By early summer all the necessary equipment was installed in the castle, and they were well into preproduction. A large ballroom filled with antiques was selected as the studio, as much for the expansive feeling of the vaulted ceiling as for the wonderful echo rebounding off the bare walls.

The soundboard and outboard gear were headquartered in an adjacent room set off through double glass doors, creating the effect of a conventional recording studio.

In a chamber on the other side of the control room, a second bank of equipment was set up, allowing the band to experiment with sounds in one room while they recorded in the other.

Eno was still a bit mystified. He had no preconceived ideas about the recording, which, as far as he was concerned, was a big plus: his mind was totally open. He also had no idea what the band wanted or expected from him. He'd taken pains to emphasize that the record wouldn't sound like anything they'd done before, and that seemed to be fine with them.

It took Eno and engineer Lanois about a week to feel comfortable with the band. But once they adapted, the album became a true collaboration. Eno and Lanois helped write songs, suggesting chord structures, musical sequences, and arrangements. After a bit of coaxing, they were even playing instruments, Lanois on bass, while Eno added a bit of keyboards.

U2's standard method of songwriting called for the band to jam, while Bono overwove melodic and lyric ideas. But this time many of the ideas they came to the castle with originated with Edge and Bono collaborating alone, laying down musical ideas on a four-track recorder and distributing cassettes to Adam and Larry. They had bits of about ten to fifteen songs when they started, but once ensconced in the castle, they quickly wrote ten or fifteen more.

Each song was built from scratch. They compared it

to the approach favored by the Beatles, with the finished product standing together as a whole while they avoided a single sound. "MLK" (about Martin Luther King), for example, developed from a study of King's life and work that Bono and Edge had undertaken, partly due to what they'd seen at the Peace Museum. "We've always had a lot of admiration for him, and for his movement. There was a need for a parallel movement in Ireland, so it's all the more poignant to us—he's not just a historical figure," Edge said.

Much of the album seemed to present itself as the inspiration of their surroundings infused the project. "Elvis Presley and America" was recorded in five minutes. Eno, working with some unrelated tracks, gave a microphone to Bono and told him to sing over the slowed-down music. Bono had never heard the piece this way and certainly had no lyric ideas for it. Five minutes later the track had beautiful melodies and ideas interwoven through it. Bono told Eno he couldn't wait to finish it. Finish it? Eno told him it was finished.

Larry and Adam were playing exceptionally well, and Bono's voice had never sounded better. Under Eno's influence, Edge found himself playing more synthesizers and piano. It quickly became apparent this wasn't to be a guitar-dominated album, though there were guitars all around. Edge worked with an arsenal of them, searching for the subtle tonal shadings that would be right for each song.

He used a Washburn acoustic guitar with a pickup for most of the initial guitar tracks. For a high-end, or "toppy," sound, he used a telecaster bought especially for the project. Despite the array of instruments at his disposal, he found none gave him the same bright, top-end treble response as the Telecaster.

Bit by bit, the album evolved.

As usual, Bono often didn't realize what his lyrics were about before they were captured on tape. It was well after the recording of "Bad," which was to become the set piece of the next tour, and the title track, "The Unforgettable Fire," that he realized both were about, among other things, heroin.

"I suppose, living on the street where I live, seeing people that I've kicked football with have their lives rearranged by this love of a drug, it just seeped subconsciously into the record."

They were finding success in their improvisatory approach. But the most successful song on the subsequent album, both commercially and artistically, as far as the band is concerned, was virtually a complete whole before U2 ever set foot in Slane Castle. This song was to be the link between their old sound and the new direction they were moving in, according to Edge. It was "Pride (In the Name of Love)."

"Pride" was originally no more than a snatch of melody and a bit of a bass part developed at a sound check and saved on cassette. Bono felt there was something in the music, and he and Edge sat around with a drum machine trying to make it into something bigger. Edge came up with a guitar line, and suddenly "We had something quite interesting." Bono had some lyric ideas, but something wasn't quite right. Originally, it was about Ronald Reagan and the ambivalent attitude toward him Bono saw in America. The "pride" was the stubborn refusal to back down, the pride that wants to build nuclear arsenals.

Then Bono remembered a conversation he'd had with an old man who told him not to try to fight darkness with light but instead to make the light shine brighter. Suddenly he realized he'd been giving Reagan too much importance. He should be singing about someone positive—Martin Luther King. As soon as the lyrical direction was changed, the song fell into place. By the time they reached Slane Castle it was demoed and ready for recording.

Edge called it the most successful pop song they'd ever written, using pop, as he said, in the best possible sense: something easily understood and accessible.

Throughout the summer Slane Castle was a beehive of

activity. A film crew came by to shoot footage for a half-hour documentary on the making of the album, focusing on the recording of "Pride." Outside the fence surrounding the manor stood fans who kept vigil while U2 recorded at Windmill Lane. Every day, twenty or so made pilgrimages to the castle, hoping for a glimpse of the band as they stepped onto the balconies for a few minutes. When the windows were opened between takes, the fans could hear music drifting outside.

In July a legendary performer came to Slane—Bob Dylan—to play at the castle's outdoor amphitheater. U2 was invited to perform but felt that due to the recording sessions, they didn't have time. That wasn't going to stop Bono from putting in a solo appearance, though.

Dylan told Bono his children were big U2 fans and invited him to the show. Midway through the set, Dylan came over to the side of the stage where Bono was standing and asked him if he knew the words to "Leopardskin Pill-Box Hat."

"Yes," Bono lied, and Dylan invited him to join him onstage for a duet. After mangling the lyrics, Bono was convinced he was finished in Dylan's book. But when it came time for the encore, Dylan's son told Bono Dad wanted the local hero to sing "Blowing in the Wind" with him. Obviously, Dylan figured everybody knew how that song went. He was wrong.

"Dylan sang all the verses I knew. It was either begin the song again or go forward. . . . I just wrote this other verse."

The creative process that worked so well inside the castle a few hundred yards away failed him now. Not only were the words wrong; Bono wasn't even singing the right tune, prompting Dylan to turn and ask his bass player what key they were in. It was something like a bad dream where you're standing naked in front of a big crowd. People didn't know what to make of Bono's performance, and he was pilloried in the following day's papers.

By the end of July, most of the recording was complete.

With mixing under way, Edge worked closely with Eno, taking out old guitar parts and overdubbing new ones, creating "guitar tapestries." With the major work finished, the band left the castle and added vocal overdubs and other finishing touches at Windmill Lane. Friends dropped by to help, including Christine Kerr, the former Chryssie Hynde, of the Pretenders, now married to Jim Kerr of the Simple Minds. Bono asked her to add background vocals.

They decided to name the album *The Unforgettable Fire*, after the images that had moved them at the Peace Museum. On the cover, they featured another castle, one a bit more run-down than Slane. It was Moydrum Castle, ivy-covered ruins in County Westmeath. Pictured on the cover of a book, *In Ruins—The Once Great Houses of Ireland*, it belonged on the cover of a record, too, U2 decided.

While the band had been busy in the studio, McGuinness had been busy in the office. Their contract with Island Records would expire soon. The music industry had had several years to take stock of U2. They knew this band would not self-destruct from drink, drugs, or ego problems. This was a band dedicated to their craft first and everything else second, a band with a growing number of fans that could be an important force in the music industry into, literally, the next century.

McGuinness closeted himself with Chris Blackwell to discuss the band's future. There were many labels that would pay tremendous amounts to acquire U2's services—not just for the profits but for the credibility they could bring to a company. Island didn't have the financial resources of some of these megalabels, but McGuinness wanted enough to make it worthwhile for the band to ignore the attractive feelers being cast in their direction. He got it. While details of U2's renewed contract have never been made public, reliable sources report that as a result of re-signing, the four lads from Dublin are now millionaires.

Their affluence seems to bring them as much distress as comfort. Bono, in particular, seems reluctant to discuss the subject. "I don't want to say that money isn't important to me. . . . I'm thankful I don't have to worry about my next meal," he's apt to say, deflecting further inquiries.

Mostly he worries about its effect on the future of U2. "It is a threat to the band, because I don't want anything to take away from our focus."

SETTING THE
WORLD ON FIRE

With *The Unforgettable Fire* finished, it was time to tour again. U2 likes to be on the road when a new album comes out. It gives them a chance to work the kinks out of new material before concert goers hear a record to compare the live versions to.

On August 29, 1984, they left Ireland for the first leg of a world tour, including their first appearance in Australia and New Zealand. Then they'd double back to Germany, Italy, France, Belgium, Holland, and Switzerland before returning for shows in Ireland and England. After that, back to the United States. It would be their most ambitious tour to date.

It seemed like ages since they'd played in front of a live audience. "The Edge had to go out and buy all our records," Bono told reporters. "He'd forgotten all his guitar parts!"

There were other technical problems to straighten out as well. They'd been concerned about recreating the intricate textures on *Unforgettable Fire* in concert and had toyed with the idea of bringing an extra musician on the road to help duplicate the layered sound of the album. After intensive discussions (and rehearsals), they decided Edge could handle the chores with the growing bank of electronic equipment he now used. The guitar hero is no longer strictly an axe man; in concert, harmonizers and digital delays vie with his guitar and echo unit for attention. Yet the devices are always subservient to the music.

"To use effects in a subtle but effective way, that's the difficult thing. It's definitely the effects you're not really aware of that are the really successful ones."

Fire Down Below

The folks Down Under had been hearing about U2 for a long time, and they were one of the most anxiously awaited groups ever to play Australia. Was it because so many Australians can trace their ancestry back to Ireland or because of U2's well-deserved reputation as one of the world's top bands? Whatever the reason, more than thirty thousand fans were waiting to see them play in Melbourne and over fifty thousand in Sydney. The crowd in Sydney didn't even seem to mind that the band came out and started playing "Gloria" in two different keys, owing to rustiness.

As usual U2 had local bands on the bill, and spent lots of time backstage talking to local musicians and making new friends. They took time to tour both cities, paying particular attention to Lady Jane Bay, Sydney's most famous nude beach, on a harbor cruise.

U2 was also eagerly awaited in New Zealand. They were favorites well before they ever showed up. In a poll in *Rip It Up*, New Zealand's top rock publication, they'd captured a host of awards, including Best Group of '83, Number 1 Album (*War*), and Bono had taken honors as Best Vocalist. "Two Hearts Beat as One" had placed #5 in the Best Single category.

While there, they dropped in on local record stores, and Bono played tapes of Romeo Void for the proprietors, informing them that this was a group whose product they would certainly want to stock.

Half a world away, "Pride (In the Name of Love)" was released at the beginning of September. After eighteen months without a new U2 record (except for the live album, which contained already-released material), people were hungry, and "Pride" jumped into the Top Twenty in England. In the first week of October, *The Unforgettable Fire* was released in England and Europe and the following week was in the number-one position. *War* and *Under a Blood Red Sky* were still on the charts, and only the week before, *October* had dropped off the top one hundred.

The next leg of their odyssey took them to Lyons, Marseilles, Toulouse, Bordeaux, Nantes, Paris, Brussels, and Rotterdam. Ten shows in two weeks. Days were spent on the bus, nights onstage. They still managed to get out and see the towns they were playing whenever they could.

U2 finally seemed to break through the language barrier, with the dates sold out long in advance. In Brussels, the audience reaction managed to set off an earthquake alarm at the Belgium Royal Observatory, though some attributed it more to the band's amplification system and Adam's bass pedals than to the crowd's wild response.

By November, with their new album at the top of the charts and eighteen months since their last English appearance, U.K. audiences were desperate for U2. Tickets were impossible to come by, except for those willing to camp out in line awaiting their sale. Opening at the Brixton Academy for two nights, they moved on to Glasgow, Edinburgh, Birmingham, and Manchester before coming back to London. By popular demand, two shows were added to the English tour at the mammoth Wembley Arena.

The Irish dates were the high points of the tour. There aren't as many people in Ireland, so the crowds aren't as big as in many other places, but nowhere else do U2 find such a feeling of family in the audience. Not surprising, since aunts, uncles, cousins, and other relatives turn out whenever U2 plays to the hometown crowd. When U2 plays Ireland it's a display of a national treasure.

Singing for Supper

They were ready to travel to the United States now and had one free day, November 25, to rest. But something important came up, and Bono wasn't about to let weariness stop him from attending to it.

On the English leg of the tour, Bono'd gotten a note from fellow-Irishman Bob Geldof, of the Boomtown Rats. Geldof had been greatly disturbed by reports of the famine sweeping Ethiopia and was trying to get some musicians together to do something about it. What he had in mind was setting up a recording session, getting the top British musicians together, and making a record whose sales would help buy food and medical supplies for the starving in Africa.

U2 was one of the first groups he contacted, and Bono immediately pledged their support for the session on November 25.

Only Bono and Adam made the one-day trip. Edge planned to be there but got sick at the last minute, while Larry, with his reclusive nature, may have felt uneasy about participating in a venture that would be crawling with members of the press.

The session was overflowing with superstars. Sting from the Police. Duran Duran. George Michael from Wham! Phil Collins. The papers called it "The greatest rock group in the world." Thirty-five stars singing together on a song called "Do They Know It's Christmas?" Following the ensemble recording, some were asked to stay and sing solos over the background of the all star choir. Bono was one of them. He also made and renewed acquaintances with Paul Weller of the Style Council, Sting, Simon le Bon, and many of the other luminaries on hand. Despite their pledge to remain apart from the glam London pop scene, Bono and Adam were moved by the spirit of cooperation and camaraderie in the Sarm West Studios that day. The only thing that impressed them more was the need to do whatever they could to help end the hunger and suffering in Ethiopia.

Adam stressed the need to keep attention on the situation. "The important thing about the whole project is that it will help to keep public interest turned on this problem and that can only be a good thing. Front page news changes daily and it'd be criminal if people forget about what's going on over there."

The only thing about the project that disturbed Bono was having to sing in front of James Taylor of Kool and the Gang, whom he considered a masterful vocalist.

By the time the single was released ten days later, U2 was already at work in America. With the help of Bono, Adam, and all the other concerned rock stars, the Band Aid project raised millions around the world to buy food and medical supplies for famine victims and helped raise the public's consciousness about world hunger. The single was the number-one song in England and Europe throughout the Christmas season.

Fanning the Flames in the United States

It had been a year and a half since U2 toured the States, and their absence intensified the debate about their substance. Were they the potential saviors of the honesty of rock 'n' roll or nothing more than naive and/or pompous schoolboys? What was their collusion with Brian Eno all about? No matter which side of the U2 fence people were on, everybody wanted answers, and they waited for *The Unforgettable Fire* to provide them. Some weren't even willing to wait that long.

In the late summer of 1984, Island Records was preparing for the U.S. release of "Pride" and *The Unforgettable Fire*.

Suddenly, disaster—as far as the record company was concerned—struck.

WLIR, the early supporter of U2 in New York, got hold of a test pressing of "Pride." Test pressings are prototype discs, made to ensure that what's on tape is the same sound that's going to be on the record. The vinyl they're pressed on isn't high quality, because they're not made to be played repeatedly.

But the test pressing sounded great to WLIR. With the questions about the band swirling around for the last year, WLIR astutely concluded that "Pride" had the power to settle the issue once and for all. Two weeks before the single was scheduled for release, the station began playing the test pressing. For an entire weekend, every hour on the hour, twenty-four hours a day, WLIR played it, to fantastic response.

Island Records was aghast. The record wouldn't be in the stores for at least two weeks. By then maybe people wouldn't be so excited, and fewer people would buy it. There was only one thing to do—Island protested and demanded WLIR stop playing the test pressing.

They needn't have worried. When the single was released, it headed straight to the Top Twenty of the college and progressive charts.

At the end of the month, when *The Unforgettable Fire* was released, all the questions about U2 seemed to have been answered. It debuted on both the college and progressive charts in the number-one position. No record had ever done that. It stayed there for eight weeks, another unprecedented achievement in the mercurial world of progressive music. The fact that U2 was still popular on these stations was remarkable. When bands go from cult to mass appeal status, like U2, trendsetters tend to write them off, charging "sell-out" and feeling that something that appeals to everybody can't be any good. But U2 was finding a new audience without leaving their old fans behind.

On December 1 they returned to America, playing at

the Tower in Philadelphia. From word on advance ticket demand around the country, it was obvious how popular they'd become since their last visit. Booked into venues that held from five to ten thousand people, they could have sold out places three times the size. But they refused to move the shows to larger halls. There'd be time for that later.

"We wanted to come in and do all the sort of smallish places that we'd played before as a sort of end to that side of it," explained Adam.

They'd be back in early 1985 for another of their three-month marathons; that's when they'd finally play the arenas. In the meantime they had other things to think about. One was their show at New York's Radio City Music Hall, on December 3.

While some call U2 a political band or a religious band, to its four members, it's nothing more or less than U2, making U2 music. But they do have strong feelings about contemporary issues, and while they don't want to get up on a soapbox, they won't shy away from what they believe in, either. Mouthing hollow proclamations and platitudes isn't enough.

One thing they believe in is the work of Amnesty International, an organization that monitors human rights abuses around the world. Through an international network, A.I. collects information on torture and oppression and tries to end these abuses by focusing attention on them. This untiring work has earned them a Nobel Peace Prize.

U2 wanted to help. Over the summer they had their American representative, Ellen Darst, contact A.I. at their headquarters in New York. The message was simple, as Mary Daly of A.I. remembers. Without the ballyhoo of a benefit concert, U2 would turn over the earnings from their next New York appearance to the organization. (They made similar arrangements to donate proceeds during their European tour in the fall.)

U2 booked Radio City for the New York appearance,

but in a bitter irony, the show that was to be a celebration of human rights was marred by incidents of abuse itself.

In retrospect, Larry says that perhaps they should have booked a bigger hall. "But how could we know?" Five thousand people had tickets, and they all wanted to get as close to the band as possible. Well before the show started, people abandoned their seats to stand at the front of the hall. The low stage, rising perhaps three feet above the floor, meant there'd be maximum contact between U2 and the audience. But it also meant you couldn't see the band if you sat in your seat, because of all the people standing up in front. The well-meaning security staff made no effort to have people return to their seats.

By the time U2 came out from the wings, a solid block of people was wedged against the stage, and more kept pushing from the back. Things were getting out of hand. Bono rescued a girl pinned in the front of the crowd, pulling her out onto the stage. The security guards, suddenly feeling overwhelmed and threatened, started scuffling with the fans. Edge dropped his guitar and leapt into the fray, trying single-handedly to separate the phalanx of security personnel from the surging crowd.

Bono continually urged the audience to move back. "If you don't stop this," he yelled, "you're not here for the same reason we are!" Finally a degree of order was restored, and with Edge back onstage, U2 began playing again. Draped in Irish flags and white standards passed up by the audience, Bono did his best to keep tempers cool, at one point asking the audience to applaud the guards for their restraint. By the time they launched into "Gloria" for the first encore, things had again gotten ugly. The security guards surged onstage, creating a human wall between the audience and U2. Bono stopped the song and ordered the guards to leave. The show ended without further incident, and a shaken U2 left the stage.

That night in their hotel, the band grappled with a disturbing realization. Their success was attracting fans who missed the point of what U2 was all about, who were oblivious to the sense of community U2 had been able to create in front of smaller audiences. Was there any way for U2 to preserve this spirit along with their growing acclaim? Or were they getting too big for their own good?

They'd gotten a brief, frightening look at the dark side of the crowd on their last tour. The glimpse had been enough to change forever the way U2 performed, certainly the way Bono did.

"People are quite aware that there's no stage big enough for me—I like to stretch the stage and I've often found myself singing from the back of the hall rather than the front," Bono had once admitted, though anyone who'd seen them play didn't need to be told.

The other three were uncomfortable with this kind of showmanship, feeling it detracted from the band as a whole. Frequently, following these expansive performances, Bono was urged, ordered, and begged to stop.

"I was getting phone calls from the band after concerts—phone calls at two in the morning where I'd have to go in and face a court martial. They were saying, 'You're either going to kill yourself, or somebody else, or the band.'"

He'd agree, only to be out in the thick of the crowd again a few nights later. Yet he'd never fully comprehended the danger of what he was doing until one night at the Los Angeles Sports Arena, a twelve-thousand-seat auditorium.

After leaving the stage, carrying the white flag into the audience, he found himself in the balcony. Suddenly he was surrounded, trapped against a wall; his white banner of peace was being ripped to shreds. There was nowhere to run to. He got into a fistfight, clawed his way to the balcony railing, and leapt into the audience twenty feet below. The crowd passed him overhead toward the stage, where he arrived almost naked and very afraid. At that moment he realized the band's fears of either him or somebody else getting killed were very real possibilities.

"It was at that stage I had to think—responsibility. I

mean, the place had gone berserk—what if somebody had died."

Since that night, Bono had remained onstage, projecting his voice and his presence instead of his body into the audience.

As Adam said, "You can't fill a large stadium physically. You have to fill it with music."

Memories of the near riot at Radio City lingered with them as they finished their tour, swinging through Washington, D.C., Toronto, Detroit, Cleveland, and Chicago, ending with shows in San Francisco and Los Angeles. An exhausted U2 got off the plane in Dublin, more than ready to take a short rest and spend Christmas at home. They'd finally broken wide open, but at what price?

Hitting the Big Time

By the end of February they were back, ready for the tour their earliest fans predicted the future held. Forty shows in more than thirty cities, stretching from New York to Honolulu, many in arena-sized venues playing to over twenty thousand fans.

Since their earliest days back in Dublin, they'd dared to believe they were meant to be one of the world's greatest groups. Few people would now disagree.

Where many bands resort to staging gimmickry, light shows, and lavish sets to make the transition from small halls to stadiums, U2 did the opposite. They wanted as many people as possible to see them play, without a lot of clutter getting in the way. The stage would be bare except for the four of them and their equipment.

"With such a clean stage, the viewer's attention isn't distracted from the people that are on it," Adam explained. "Even the smallest movement comes across in that kind of setup."

They were still the hardworking band they were when

they crossed the Atlantic for their first low-budget tours, but now they could afford first-class accommodations and travel arrangements.

For the Florida dates, they set up headquarters in a hotel on Marco Island, a resort on the Gulf Coast, and helicoptered to gigs around the state, taking the opportunity to relax in the sun between shows.

They were being taken seriously by more than just the rock world. Publications like *The Wall Street Journal* and the *Christian Science Monitor* now reported the U2 phenomenon. U2 sold out Madison Square Garden, where they long ago said they deserved to play, in two hours. In Providence, Rhode Island, fans camped out overnight in subfreezing weather to be first in line for tickets. And so it was as they worked their way around the country.

The sold-out shows were particularly impressive considering U2 was still a band without a hit single. "Pride" had briefly moved into the Top Thirty before moving back down the singles charts.

"Obviously it would be great to have a hit," Adam observed. "But it would have to be with a song that was worthwhile. I think 'Pride' should have been a hit. The whole band was disappointed that it didn't do better here."

But there were other accolades. In March, *Rolling Stone* magazine featured U2 on the cover, with the headline "Our Choice: Band of the '80s." The adulatory account summed up the situation, saying, "For a growing number of rock 'n' roll fans, U2...has become the band that matters most, maybe even the only band that matters."

The Unforgettable Fire was now number 15 on the U.S. album charts. More shows were added to the tour to accommodate the demand for tickets.

U2 transformed the shows in these massive halls into close-knit spiritual experiences. At every down tempo song, the audience was a sea of lighted matches, reflecting the spark and the glow emanating from the stage.

"Does anyone here play guitar?" Bono would ask the crowd near the end of the set, and pick one of the hundreds with their hands raised to be a temporary member of U2. Bono gave the draftee an acoustic guitar and told him or her what to play, saying, "These are the four most important chords in the world." The rest of the band would join in and deliver a stirring rendition of Dylan's "Knocking on Heaven's Door."

With their acclaim reaching megastatus, they were constantly aware of the danger of the crowd's enthusiasm getting out of hand, as it had at Radio City. It was a danger they couldn't always control, no matter how positive the message in their music. They weren't even sure the audiences attracted by their newfound mass appeal realized there was a message. Adam admitted that it was probably "alarmingly true" that many of their young fans didn't even know who Martin Luther King, Jr., was.

In Phoenix they had their hands full trying to prevent a riot of pushing and shoving among the twenty thousand fans at the Compt Terrace facility. To calm the audience, Bono put U2's music to the ultimate test, calling for the band to play "Pride" in the middle of the set, the song they usually played as an encore on the tour. It wasn't enough. Spotting one aggressive fan who was pushing and punching everyone nearby, Bono summoned him onto the stage.

"I saw what you did," he screamed at the fan. "You get out of here. I don't ever want to see you at one of our concerts again." Bono had security guards eject the troublemaker from the hall.

Looking back on the show the next day, he remarked, "Survival was the theme of the evening." Again, some people were missing the point of the music, reducing U2 to a mere rock 'n' roll band.

"When the energy of the crowd is so brutal, the spirit of the music flees, and all you're left with is crashing drums and clanging guitars."

Fortunately these incidents were few and far between. Most of the wildly enthusiastic audiences shared U2's beliefs in music and in people.

When the tour ended at the Hollywood, Florida, Sportatorium on May 3, 1985, they'd played before half a million people. *War* and *The Unforgettable Fire* had gone platinum. *Under a Blood Red Sky* and *October* were certified gold. And all were still riding the album charts. America had been conquered.

U2 returned home, spending the summer playing European concerts and outdoor festivals. The high point was a joyous reunion with their hometown fans in Dublin's Croke Park on June 29. Now not even Phoenix Park was big enough for them.

The end of May saw the release of a four-song EP, *Wide Awake in America*, containing live versions of "Bad" and "A Sort of Homecoming," along with two previously unreleased studio cuts, "Love Comes Tumbling" and "Three Sunrises," the first produced by U2, the second recorded with Eno at Slane Castle.

There was also, of course, their participation in perhaps the greatest collaborative event in rock history— the Live Aid concert on July 13, staged simultaneously in Philadelphia's JFK Stadium in the United States and London's Wembley Arena in England. U2 joined their friends from the original Band Aid recording in London, along with many new additions from the Who's Who in rockdom, raising money and public consciousness to help defeat hunger. U2's set at Wembley was among the most heartfelt and uplifting.

After opening with "Sunday Bloody Sunday", they launched into "Bad", using the instrumental break to segue into a medley of Lou Reed's "Satellite of Love" and "Walk on the Wild Side", and the Stone's "Goodbye, Ruby Tuesday". Later, they came back for the ensemble singing of "Do They Know It's Chrismas?", with Bono in a featured role. Their inspiring and galvanized performance convinced the millions who'd never seen them before what their fans have known all along— There is no other band in the world like U2.

APPENDIXES

PROFILES

Bono
Singer

Paul Hewson, a.k.a. Bono, born May 10, 1960, is U2's most vocal and visual presence. His most enduring and endearing trait is his loquatiousness. Bono has never in his life been at a loss for words.

Not wishing to confine his conversation to English, he's interested in foreign languages, too, particularly French, Spanish, and Gaelic, which he regrets he didn't take the time to study properly in high school.

Known for the political verses he himself writes, he collects foreign poetry, specializing in African, Indian, and French verse.

He describes his political affiliation as "aggressive pacifist."

He loves movies. Among his favorites: *The Tin Drum, If, Alfie, Lord of the Flies, The Graduate, Monty Python and the Holy Grail*. Kim Novak is his favorite movie star. He tries to keep up with the latest films by ducking into theaters whenever he can on tour. Needless to say, this means he doesn't get to see very many movies.

His favorite books are the Bible, *Lord of the Flies*,

The Rise and Fall of Western Civilization and Thought, the *Oxford Companion to English Literature*, *One Flew Over the Cuckoo's Nest*.

Favorite foods: Cornflakes and pecan pie.

He likes to watch TV, particularly "Hawaii Five-O," "Hall's Pictorial Weekly" (you'll have to go to Ireland to see it), and "Skippy the Bush Kangaroo" (go to England for this one).

Of course, he also loves music. Faves: *The Wild, The Innocent and The E Street Shuffle* (Bruce Springsteen), "Happy Xmas (War Is Over)" (John Lennon) [Bono's first single], "Hello Hurray" (Alice Cooper) [his second single], "Alternative Ulster" (Stiff Little Fingers), "Faithfully Departed" (Radiators from Space), "Better Scream" (Wah!), "In the Grey Light" (Virgin Prunes) [his pals since childhood], *Ol' Blue Eyes* (F. Sinatra), theme from *Midnight Express*, theme from *The Good, the Bad, and the Ugly*.

The Edge
Guitar

Dave Evans, a.k.a. the Edge, or just plain Edge, born August 8, 1961, is U2's guitarist *extraordinaire*. Yet for all his instrumental prowess, he isn't "into" his guitar; that is, when the show's over, he packs it up and forgets about it. He's never been one to spend hours doodling away and honing his chops. It comes naturally to him.

The Edge is as reserved and dignified as Bono is outgoing and talkative. He favors shirts buttoned up to the neck and rarely cracks a smile. When he does, it lights up a whole room.

Married, with a young daughter named Holly, Edge prefers spending the little time he has to himself at home with his family. His hobby is video, and he's learning the intricacies of video recording with the same analytical precision he applied to guitar. He likes to take a video camera on the road, recording everything he sees with the dedication of an aspiring filmmaker. He's already applying his newfound skills to U2's music videos.

He also loves skiing, but unfortunately, with so much riding on his health, tour-insurance underwriters frown upon his sporting on the slopes, and he's had to greatly curtail this favorite pastime as a result.

Some of his favorite music:

"Born under Punches (The Heat Goes On)" (Talking Heads); "State of Independence" (Donna Summer); "Fields of Fire" (Big Country); "Someone Somewhere in the Summertime" (Simple Minds); "Holidays in the Sun" (Sex Pistols); "My Jamaican Guy" (Grace Jones); "The Stand" (The Alarm), "Chill Out" (Black Uhuru).

Adam Clayton
Bass

Adam Clayton, born March 13, 1960, has frequently been described as U2's token hedonist. Yet beneath the fun-loving exterior lies a serious musician and businessman. During their formative years Adam managed the band and proved himself a tireless and skillful hustler in the best sense of the word. Even now he remains aware of the fine points of contracts, operating costs, and other minutiae of U2's business.

He still engages in a bit of harmless carousing on the road, often staying up till all hours at night. Perhaps this is why he also displays such a fondness for coffee, insisting on several cups every morning.

He lives in a house in Dublin and, when not on the road, can usually be found inside it, where his favorite pastimes include watching TV and dining on home-cooked meals.

He professes to have mainstream musical tastes, singling out Sade, Springsteen, and George Thurogood. When he's on the road he usually takes along well over a hundred cassettes to keep him company.

His clothing preferences are changeable, going from dark, simple garments to bright tie-dyed tank tops and bracelets, depending on his mood.

Larry Mullen, Jr.
Drums

Larry Mullen, Jr. (the others call him Lawrence when they want to get on his case), born October 31, 1961, is the youngest and most private member of U2. That's not an easy distinction to win in a band whose members like to keep their personal lives personal and constantly deflect attempts to build a cult of personality around them.

Generally Larry refuses to speak to members of the press. Some interpret this as shyness, but this isn't the case at all. He's very self-assured and simply doesn't want to be bothered answering the same questions all the time.

While the others are meeting the press, he's often at the hotel playing his acoustic guitar.

He has a quick and ready sense of humor but at the same time is very fussy about things, particularly his drum setup, and won't hesitate to give someone a piece of his mind when disturbed.

Among his musical influences, he cites jazz drummers in general and John Bonham in particular. He's generous and willing to share whatever he has. On tour, he provides the drummers of U2's support bands with enough drumsticks to last a year and is keen on discussing percussion hardware and technique.

His dress style is modern motorcycle: Denim trousers, white tee-shirts, leather jackets, and shades. He usually sports a single earring in his left ear and a cross around his neck.

His father recently remarried, his mother having died some years ago, and at last report Larry still lived at home, though he had the financial wherewithal to relocate some time ago.

He has been teased by fellow band members for being superstitious. Traveling through France, the others were able to mildly unnerve him at one stop by insisting they'd given a fan his birthdate, allowing her to cast a spell on him.

Mullen seems uncomfortable with U2's fame and customarily doesn't grant interviews. In the individual portraits on the back of the recent EP *Wide Awake in America*, he managed to completely obscure his features by keeping his face hidden in shadows.

DISCOGRAPHY

Singles

Another Day/Twilight 3/80
11 O'Clock Tick Tock/Touch 5/80
A Day without Me/Things to Make and Do 8/80
I Will Follow/Boy-Girl 10/80
Fire/J. Swallo 7/81
Gloria/I Will Follow 9/81
A Celebration/Trash Trampoline and Party Girl 3/82
New Year's Day/Treasure 1/83
Two Hearts Beat as One/Endless Sleep 3/83
New Year's Day/Two Hearts Beat as One 3/83
Pride (In the Name of Love)/Boomerang II 9/84
4th of July/Boomerang II 9/84

EPs

U2 Three Out of Control/Stories for Boys/Boy-
Girl 11/79

Just for Kicks (Compilation of Top Dublin Bands)
Includes Stories for Boys 1/80

*Cry/The Electric Co./11 O'Clock Tick Tock/
The Ocean* 7/81

4 U2 Play U2 Three/Another Day/11 O'Clock Tick
Tock/I Will Follow 9/82

*Fire/I Threw a Brick through a Window/A
Day without Me* 1/83

*Two Hearts Beat as One/New Year's Day/
Two Hearts Beat as One* 3/83

Wide Awake in America Bad/A Sort of
Homecoming/Three Sunrises/Love Comes
Tumbling 5/85

Albums

Boy 1980

Side I
I Will Follow
Twilight
An Cat Dubh
Into the Heart
Out of Control

Side II
Stories for Boys
The Ocean
A Day without Me
Another Time, Another Place
The Electric Co.
Shadows and Tall Trees

October 1981

Side I
Gloria
I Fall Down
I Threw a Brick through a Window
Rejoice
Fire

Side II
Tomorrow
October
With a Shout
Stranger in a Strange Land
Scarlet
Is That All

War 1983

Side I
Sunday Bloody Sunday
Seconds
New Year's Day
Like a Song
Drowning Man

Side II
The Refugee

Two Hearts Beat as One
Red Light
Surrender
40

Under a Blood Red Sky 1983

Side I
Gloria
11 O'Clock Tick Tock
I Will Follow
Trash Trampoline and Party Girl

Side II
Sunday Bloody Sunday
The Electric Co.
New Year's Day
40

The Unforgettable Fire 1984

Side I
A Sort of Homecoming
Pride (In the Name of Love)
Fire
The Unforgettable Fire
Promenade

Side II
4th of July
Bad
Indian Summer Sky
Elvis Presley and America
MLK

EQUIPMENT

The Edge

Guitars

Fender Stratocaster '71
Gibson Explorer '76
Fender Telecaster '61
Les Paul Deluxe
Gretsch Falcon '59 (Stereo pickups rewired to mono)
Washburn Acoustic
Epiphone Lap Steel (Found at Gruhn Guitars, Nashville)

Strings

Superwound Selectras (.011 or .012–.056)

Keyboards

Yamaha CP 70 Electric Piano
Yamaha DX7 Synthesizer

Oberheim OB-8
Oberheim DSX

Amplifiers

Vox AC30 (12-inch speakers)
Mesa Boogies (MK-11 C series)
Roland JC 120 amp

Effects

Memory Man Echo Unit
Boss SDC 700 Effects Selector
Korg SDD 3000 Digital Delays
Electro Harmonix Memory Man Analog Delay
Yamaha R-1000 Digital Reverb
Yamaha D-15 Digital Delay
MXR Pitch Transposer
MXR Compressor
Boss TU-12 Tuner

Adam

Guitars

Fender Precision
Ibanez Musician
Fender Jazz Bass

Amplifiers

Alembic Pre-amp
Ampeg SVT Bass Head
Harbinger Cabinets (4 15-inch Gauss Speakers)
JBL 2410 High Frequency Drivers
BGW 750B
BGW 250B

Effects

Boss SDC 700 Effects Selector
Furman Parametric Equalizer
Moog Taurus Pedals
Ibanez UE 400 Digital Delay
Ibanez HD 1000 Digital Delay
Nady 700 Wireless Cable System

Larry

Drums

Yamaha Power Recording Series Drums
24-inch bass
14-inch Rack Tom
2 16-inch Floor Toms
18-inch Floor Tom
14 × 6½-inch Snare
Ludwig Piccolo Snare
Eddie Ryan Piccolo Snare
2 Lapin Timbales

Cymbals

Paiste 2002 18-inch Crash
2 Rude 18-inch Crash
20-inch Rude Crash
2002 20-inch Chinatop
14-inch Sound Edge Hi-hat

Yamaha Hardware
Evans Drum Heads
Sticks: Designed by Capella Wood, New Jersey

Effects

Simmons SDS7 (Triggered by Acoustic Drums)
Oberheim DX Click Track

Bono

Shure SM-57 Microphone
Shure SM-58 Microphone
Clair Brothers Sound System

When you have someone in your band like the Edge, you don't need another guitar player. (Of course, if you have a singer like Bono, you don't need two guitars either.) But every so often Bono will strap on an axe to add some rhythm coloration.

Guitar: Fender Lead II
Amplifier: Roland Bolt 60

VIDEOGRAPHY

Gloria 1982
Celebration 1982
New Year's Day 1983
Two Hearts Beat as One 1983
Sunday Bloody Sunday/11 O'Clock Tick Tock/I Will Follow (from Red Rocks performance) 1984
Under a Blood Red Sky (sixty-minute video of Red Rocks performance) 1984
Pride (In the Name of Love) 1984
Pride (In the Name of Love)—(Donald Kamel version) 1984
The Unforgettable Fire (thirty-minute documentary) 1984
A Sort of Homecoming 1984

EARLY SONGS

*U*2's put many great songs on record. But many fine compositions never made it to vinyl. Here are the names of some of them:

The Dream Is Over
Jack in the Box
Night Fright
Street Missions
Concentration Cramp
Inside Out
Hang Up!
Judith
Trevor (became Touch)
The Magic Carpet
Walk Away
Alone in the Night
Silver Lining (became 11 O'Clock Tick Tock)
Cartoon World
The King's New Clothes

FAN CLUB INFORMATION

North America

U2 Info
P.O. Box 156
Princeton Junction, New Jersey, 08550
U.S.A.
   S.A.S.E.

Europe

U2 Info
P.O. Box 48
London, N. 6
England
   S.A.E.

ABOUT THE AUTHOR

*B*orn in the Belgian Congo, Winston Brandt was an explorer and naturalist before moving to New York, where he works as a writer and musician.